Teacher's Guide

PATHWAYS

Reading, Writing, and Critical Thinking

4

Nancy Hubley

Mari Vargo

Laurie Blass

Keith S. Folse, Series Consultant

 NATIONAL GEOGRAPHIC LEARNING |  HEINLE CENGAGE Learning

Australia • Brazil • Japan • Korea • Mexico • Singapore • Spain • United Kingdom • United States

Pathways 4 Teacher's Guide

Publisher: Andrew Robinson

Executive Editor: Sean Bermingham

Associate Development Editor: Ridhima Thakral

Development Editor: Karen Davy

Director of Global Marketing: Ian Martin

Director of Content and Media Production: Michael Burggren

Sr. Content Project Manager: Daisy Sosa

Manufacturing Buyer: Marybeth Hennebury

Cover Design: Page 2 LLC

Cover Image: Alaska Stock Images/ National Geographic Creative

Interior Design: Page 2 LLC, Cenveo Publisher Services/Nesbitt Graphics, Inc.

Composition: Cenveo Publisher Services/ Nesbitt Graphics, Inc.

ISBN-13: 978-1-133-31741-8

National Geographic Learning
20 Channel Center St.
Boston, MA 02210
USA

Cengage Learning is a leading provider of customized learning solutions with office locations around the globe, including Singapore, the United Kingdom, Australia, Mexico, Brazil, and Japan. Locate your local office at: **international.cengage.com/region**

Cengage Learning products are represented in Canada by Nelson Education, Ltd.

Visit National Geographic Learning online at **NGL.cengage.com**
Visit our corporate website at **www.cengage.com**

Printed in the United States of America
1 2 3 4 5 6 7 8   19 18 17 16 15 14

TABLE OF CONTENTS

Advantages of *Pathways Reading, Writing, and Critical Thinking*

In *Pathways Reading, Writing, and Critical Thinking*, real-world content from *National Geographic* publications provides a context for meaningful language acquisition. Students learn essential, high-frequency vocabulary, review important grammatical structures, and practice reading and writing skills that will allow them to succeed in academic settings.

Pathways Reading, Writing, and Critical Thinking can be used in a wide variety of language-learning programs, from high schools and community colleges to private language institutes and intensive English programs. The high-interest content motivates students and teachers alike.

The following features are included in *Pathways Reading, Writing, and Critical Thinking*:

- Academic Pathways goals at the beginning of each unit give students and teachers clear performance objectives.

- Opening pages introduce the unit theme and provide key vocabulary and concepts.

- Readings in a variety of academic content areas and genres present target vocabulary and provide ideas for writing.

- An audio program includes recordings of all the reading texts.

- Clear grammar charts present key structures and language for writing assignments.

- An *Independent Student Handbook* and Vocabulary Index serve as tools to use in class or for self-study and review.

Teaching Language Skills and Academic Literacy

Students need more than language skills to succeed in an academic setting. In addition to teaching the English language, the *Pathways* series teaches academic literacy, which includes not only reading, writing, speaking, and listening skills, but also visual literacy, classroom participation and collaboration skills, critical thinking, and the ability to use technology for learning. Students today are expected to be motivated, inquisitive, original, and creative. In short, they're expected to possess quite an extensive skills set before they even begin their major course of study.

Using *National Geographic* Content in a Language Class

The use of high-interest content from real *National Geographic* publications sets the *Pathways* series apart. Students are engaged by fascinating stories about real people and places around the world and the important issues that affect us all.

High-interest reading passages provide opportunities to practice reading and critical thinking skills, while providing vocabulary and ideas for writing assignments.

The topics in *Pathways Reading, Writing, and Critical Thinking* correspond to academic subject areas and appeal to a wide range of interests. For example:

Academic Subject Area	Unit Title	Unit Theme
Environmental Science/Life Science	*Conservation and Protection*	the worldwide decline in the population of big cats, and what can be done to save them
Sociology/Aesthetics	*Beautiful*	the principles that underlie concepts of beauty, and the six elements that characterize great photographs
Life Science/Sociology	*Working Together*	swarm intelligence, or the idea that when animals, people, and robots work together cooperatively, there are advantages for both individuals and the group
History/Economics	*Resources and Development*	an exploration of development by examining the geography and history of Africa
Health and Medicine	*Living Longer*	the issue of longevity is explored, focusing especially on societies where a number of people live healthy lives into their 90s and beyond

Increasing Visual Literacy

Photographs, maps, charts, and graphs can all convey enormous amounts of information. Lecturers and professors rarely present information without some kind of visual aid. Helping students to make sense of visuals is an important part of preparing them for academic success.

Where and How We Live

The map shows population density; the brightest points are the highest densities. Each country is colored according to its average annual gross national income per capita, using categories established by the World Bank. Some nations—such as economic powerhouses China and India—have an especially wide range of incomes. But as the two most populous countries, both are lower middle class when income is averaged per capita.

Maps are used in the *Pathways* series not only to show locations and geographical features, but also to illustrate historical facts and current trends—both local and global. In an academic setting, the ability to read maps is expected, and *Pathways* gives students opportunities to hone that skill.

Charts and graphs present numerical data in a visual way, and the *Pathways* series gives students practice in reading them.

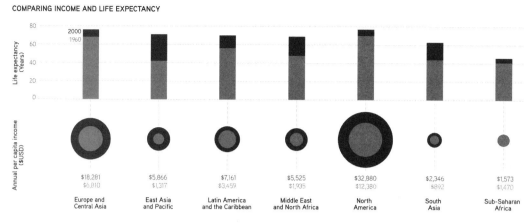

COMPARING INCOME AND LIFE EXPECTANCY

Pathways uses a variety of graphic organizers to present content. Graphic organizers appeal to visual learners by showing relationships between ideas in a visual way. Students use graphic organizers for a number of reading and writing tasks such as note taking, comparing similarities and differences, brainstorming, identifying main ideas and details, and organizing notes for writing assignments.

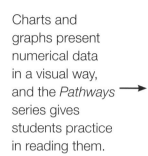

The Elements of a Beautiful Photograph

light
↓
reveals subject; makes everything else visible: e.g., color, form
↓
Abell photo: light gives personality to trees

In addition to the more standard pie charts and bar graphs, *Pathways* includes other stimulating informational visuals from *National Geographic* publications.

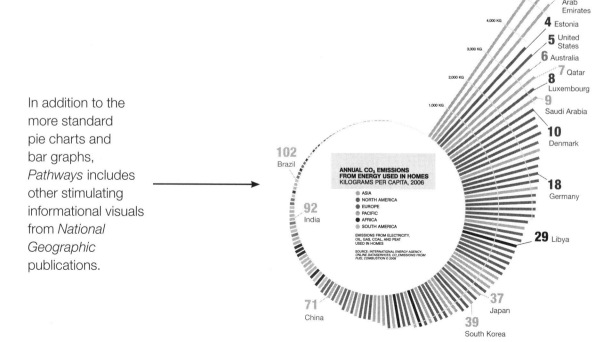

ANNUAL CO₂ EMISSIONS FROM ENERGY USED IN HOMES
KILOGRAMS PER CAPITA, 2006

Building Critical Thinking Skills

Critical thinking skills are explicitly taught and practiced in *Pathways Reading, Writing, and Critical Thinking*. Critical thinking—the ability to make judgments and decisions based on evidence and reason—is an essential skill for students in an academic setting, where they're expected to reflect on and analyze information rather than simply remember it. Students need to be prepared to think critically while listening, reading, writing, and participating in discussions.

The ability to think critically also contributes to language acquisition by requiring deep processing of the language. Having to consider an idea in relation to other ideas and then articulate a response or an opinion about it involves making complex associations in the brain. This thought process in turn leads to better comprehension and retention of the target language.

Here are just a few examples of the academic tasks that require critical thinking skills:

- deciding which material from a reading to take notes on
- determining a writer's purpose when assessing the content of a reading
- forming an opinion on an issue based on facts and evidence
- relating new information to one's personal experiences
- giving specific examples to support one's main idea
- evaluating sources of information
- synthesizing information

The *Pathways* series gives explicit instruction and practice of critical thinking skills. Each unit has a Critical Thinking Focus and several practice exercises. For example:

 E | Critical Thinking: Analyzing Evidence. In the reading on pages 6–12, what evidence does the writer present in support of either side of the main issue? Take notes in the chart. Then discuss answers to the questions below with a partner.

Issue: Our impact on the planet is so great that we are now living in a new epoch.	
Arguments For	**Arguments Against**

Using Video in the Language Classroom

The video clips in *Pathways Reading, Writing, and Critical Thinking* come from the award-winning *National Geographic* film collection and act as a bridge between Lessons A and B of each unit. The videos present another perspective on the unit theme in a visually dynamic way. The narration for each video has been carefully graded to feature vocabulary items and structures that are appropriate for students' proficiency level.

Teaching video-viewing skills

In daily life, nonfiction videos can be found on television, on the Internet, and in movie theaters in the form of documentaries. Just as *Pathways* provides a wide variety of reading passages to build students' reading skills, the series also builds viewing skills with videos from *National Geographic*. *Pathways* promotes visual and digital literacy so learners can competently use a wide range of modern media.

Videos differ from reading texts in important ways. First, students are processing information by viewing and listening simultaneously. Visual images include information about the video's setting as well as clues found in nonverbal communication, such as facial expressions, gestures, and other body language. The video may also include maps and diagrams to explain information and processes. The soundtrack contains narration, conversations, music, and sound effects. Some contextual words may appear on screen in signs or as identification of people or settings. In addition, full English subtitles are available as a teaching and learning option.

The Viewing section

The viewing section in each unit features activities for students to do before, while, and after they watch the video.

Before Viewing prepares students for the video by activating their background knowledge and stimulating interest in the topic. Some effective ways of previewing include

- brainstorming ideas and discussing what the class already knows about the topic;
- using photographs and the video's title to predict the content;
- pre-teaching key vocabulary essential to understanding the video content.

While Viewing tasks allow students to focus on

- checking their predictions;
- identifying the main ideas;
- watching and listening for particular details;
- watching and listening for opinions and inferences;
- observing gestures, body language, and other non-verbal communication.

After Viewing gives students opportunities to check comprehension and relate the video to other aspects of the unit by

- describing the main points or sequence of events;
- answering questions to check comprehension of main ideas and key information;
- synthesizing information from the video and previous reading material on the topic.

Some options for using the videos

Preview each video before presenting it in class to become familiar with the content, anticipate questions students might have, and plan how to exploit the video most effectively. See individual units in this Teacher's Guide for notes and suggestions for teaching each video.

Here are some techniques for using video in class:

- Have students preview the video by reading the transcript in the back of the student textbook.
- Pause, rewind, or fast-forward the video to focus on key segments or events.
- Pause the video and ask students to predict what will happen next. Resume the video so students can check their predictions.
- Have students watch the video, or parts of the video, with the sound off so they can focus on what they see. Have students share their ideas about the content. Then play the video with the sound on so students can check their ideas.
- After students have watched the video with the sound on, have them watch again with sound off. Pause the video in different places and ask students to retell the information in their own words.
- Have students watch first without subtitles and discuss the main ideas. Then play the video again with subtitles so students can check their ideas.
- Have students watch the video with the subtitles to help with unknown vocabulary and to aid comprehension.
- Have students watch the video independently and complete the activities in the Online Workbook.

As an optional special project, have students make a presentation or create a written report about a video of their choice, using language they have learned from the textbook and the video narration.

Video scripts are printed in the back of the student textbook. All video clips are on the Online Workbook, the Presentation Tool CD-ROM, and on the classroom DVD. The Online Workbook also contains additional activities about the video.

Features of the *Pathways* Teacher's Guide

The *Pathways* Teacher's Guide contains teaching notes, answer keys, reading and video overviews, and warm-up and extension activities to help teachers present the material in the student textbook.

Ideas for... Boxes

Throughout the *Pathways* Teacher's Guide, there are three main types of *Ideas for. . .* Boxes:

- **Ideas for Checking Comprehension** present additional questions for assessing students' comprehension of the reading texts.

- **Ideas for Expansion** suggest ways to expand on the content of the book when students need extra instruction or when they have a high level of interest in a topic.

- **Ideas for Further Research** give suggestions for Web sites or other sources of information when students want to learn more about a topic.

Tips

Tips for instruction and classroom management are provided throughout the *Pathways* Teacher's Guide. The tips are especially helpful to less-experienced teachers, but they are also a resource for more-experienced teachers, providing new ideas and adding variety to the classroom routine.

Suggested Time Frames

The main sections of Lessons A and B in the Teacher's Guide contain small clock icons with suggested times for completing the various tasks. The Writing Task sections in Lesson B do not have time icons because students will likely do writing assignments independently, outside of class. The times are intended as suggestions and may vary, depending on particular teaching situations. Similarly, the estimated time for completing a unit is between four and five class hours. This estimate may vary, depending on how much material is presented in class, given as homework, or other factors.

Graphic Organizers

A set of ten graphic organizers is included in the back of the Teacher's Guide (pages 101–110). You can photocopy these organizers as optional ways to help students organize information as they read particular reading texts or watch certain videos in the units.

Audio Program

The audio program includes recordings of all the reading passages in the student textbook. As an option, you may have students listen to the recordings while they read.

Following are some frequently asked questions about the *Pathways Reading, Writing, and Critical Thinking* series, answered by authors Laurie Blass and Mari Vargo.

1. How are the Student Book units organized?

Each unit in *Pathways Reading, Writing, and Critical Thinking 4* consists of two lessons: A and B. Lesson A focuses on reading and Lesson B on writing. A video viewing segment between Lessons A and B serves as a bridge between the two lessons and offers another perspective on the unit theme. Together, these lessons take students from an introduction to the unit theme, through a series of structured reading, vocabulary, and critical thinking activities, and finally through a guided writing assignment that synthesizes the skills, topics, and language presented in the unit.

2. What is the purpose of the Opening and Exploring the Theme pages?

The Opening page presents the unit goals—the Academic Pathways—and provides a general introduction to the unit theme through discussion questions. Exploring the Theme pages are springboards for students to interact with photographs and other graphical information such as maps, graphs, and charts. These pages get students thinking critically and sharing ideas about the unit theme. They present each unit's key concepts and vocabulary while providing opportunities for students to develop visual literacy skills.

3. How does *Pathways Reading, Writing, and Critical Thinking* develop reading strategies?

Each Lesson A presents an academic reading skill along with a series of practice activities. These skills include identifying main and supporting ideas, interpreting visual information, identifying sequence, scanning for specific information, and using graphic organizers to take notes.

4. How does the series develop critical thinking skills?

Critical thinking skills are explicitly taught and practiced in *Pathways Reading, Writing, and Critical Thinking*. Each Lesson A includes a specific CT (critical thinking) Focus box that explains the skill—often modeling the thinking process required by the skill through a series of questions. Critical thinking skills include making inferences, evaluating sources for reliability, reading literature critically, and analyzing text organization. Students apply the reading skill to the passage in Lesson A.

In addition, there are multiple opportunities throughout each unit for students to practice synthesizing information—relating and connecting ideas from different parts of the unit—an essential skill for academic success. Students synthesize and apply information from the video and the Lesson A reading, which also prepares them for the unit's writing assignment.

5. How does the series build vocabulary skills?

A set of academic and high-frequency vocabulary items is targeted in Lesson A. Students acquire and reinforce their knowledge of these items by identifying them in context, guessing their meaning, and using them in activities that reinforce meaning and usage. These target words are reinforced and recycled throughout the series. In addition, Word Partners and Word Link boxes in Lesson A expand students' working vocabulary. Word Partners boxes show high-frequency patterns, or collocations, in which target words appear. Word Link boxes focus on prefixes, suffixes, and roots associated with target words.

Vocabulary for Writing activities in Lesson B provide words and phrases that students can use in their writing. This vocabulary is specifically related to the writing topic or genre.

6. What is the writing process approach taken in this series?

In acquiring academic writing skills, students need to learn early on that writing is re-writing. This is the premise of the process approach to writing, and the approach taken by *Pathways Reading, Writing, and Critical Thinking*. Accordingly, as students work through the pre-writing, writing, and post-writing activities in each unit, they draft and re-draft their assignments. Repeating this process as they progress through the units, students internalize the steps and gradually become more independent writers.

7. How does it develop writing skills?

The writing section of each unit begins with a presentation of the writing goal, and then proceeds through the writing process: gathering ideas, planning, drafting, revising, and editing. Students follow this process in a step-by-step manner, working through a series of structured activities. For example, they use outlines and graphic organizers in the planning stage, answer focused questions in the revision stage, and use a checklist in the editing stage.

Each Lesson B includes a Writing Skill presentation box along with a series of practice activities. These presentations include essay-writing skills such as writing a thesis statement, supporting a thesis statement, and writing introductions and conclusions. In the later units, students learn how to prepare and write a research paper and write critically about literature. Students practice by evaluating model essays and then apply what they've learned to their own essays.

In addition, each Lesson B includes a Language for Writing presentation that highlights a lexical or grammar point specifically useful for that unit's writing assignment. Examples include adding information with verbal phrases, referring to sources, and explaining the significance of evidence. Students practice the structure in an activity, and then apply what they've learned to their own essays as they write and edit their work.

8. What are some things to keep in mind when using the writing process?

In the brainstorming stage, students work with partners. This helps them express and clarify their ideas before they begin to write. In this stage, remind students that they should not monitor themselves or each other in any way. That is, ideas should flow freely without criticism or limitation.

As part of the brainstorming stage, students complete a timed, free-writing activity. This activity should be done in class, if possible, so you can time it. The free-writing activity is a fluency exercise—that is, the focus is on generating ideas. Accordingly, remind students not to worry about grammar, spelling, or punctuation. The goal is to record ideas in a fluent manner. Do not correct or grade free-writing exercises. If you collect them, you may want to write supportive, constructive comments on students' ideas.

The editing phase includes a peer evaluation activity that encourages students to give each other positive feedback at the outset. Reinforce the idea that students should read their partner's draft first just for meaning and to find at least one positive thing to say about the ideas in the essay. If necessary, provide students with some positive conversation starters such as "I like the way you explain X." "Your idea about X is interesting." Remind them of some ways to soften suggestions, such as: "You might want to . . . " "You could . . . ."

9. How are reading and writing integrated in the series?

All the lessons in each unit of *Pathways Reading, Writing, and Critical Thinking* are thematically linked. Lesson A readings and activities present and reinforce vocabulary, language, and ideas that students will use in their writing assignments. In addition, Lesson A readings and skill presentations often model the genre that students will be writing in Lesson B. For example, in Unit 3, students read about photography in the Lesson A passage and write about a visual art form in Lesson B. In Unit 9 they learn to analyze a personal narrative in Lesson A and write their own extended personal narrative in Lesson B.

Our Human Impact

Academic Track
Interdisciplinary

Academic Pathways:
Lesson A: Understanding cohesion
　　　　　Analyzing arguments
Lesson B: Reviewing essay writing
　　　　　Writing a cause-effect essay

UNIT 1

Unit Theme

Unit 1 explores the controversial idea that humans have such a powerful impact on planet Earth that their activities will leave a mark on the geological record. Thus, some scientists argue, we should rename the current geological period the Anthropocene (pronounced *an THROW poe seen*).

5 mins

Think and Discuss *(page 1)*

- Ask students to describe the photo. Ask: *What do you see in the photo? What activity is going on here? Where can you find places like this?* (Such terraces are found in east, south, and southeast Asia and the Andes mountain range in South America.)

- Discuss the concept of terrace agriculture. *Why do people go to great effort to reshape the land?* (It makes it possible to grow crops on hilly land, it prevents erosion, and it uses water carefully.)

- Discuss possible answers to questions 1 and 2. Students may mention dams on rivers, reclaimed land, cutting down forests, mining, and the massive use of artificial fertilizers for agriculture, all of which have advantages and disadvantages. (For example, cutting down forests provides us with wood, but it also takes away some animals' habitat.)

- Discuss the meaning of the unit title and how it might relate to the photo.

15 mins

Exploring the Theme
(pages 2–3)

- The opening spread features a world map showing human impact by large cities, pollution, desertification, and deforestation. Boxes provide additional information about the last three topics.

- Draw students' attention to the map key on the left side as well as the inset map on the right.

- The questions in section A are answered by using the map key. Ask students to support their answers using the key.

- Discuss question 2, asking about the size of megacities (populations of over 10 million) and how they are shown on the map. Have students identify the megacities on each continent. Are there any surprises? (There are no megacities in Western Europe.)

- Discuss question 3. (For pollution, note the outlines for land affected by acid rain as well as the shipping lanes in the oceans. The markings for former forest can be seen most clearly in Scandinavia.)

- For question 4, students use the color coding of the inset map to identify places where human impact is greatest and least.

- Use the questions in section B to lead into a general discussion of the human impact in developed and less developed countries.

Answer Key

Possible answers:

1. city size, pollution, desertification, and deforestation
2. Megacities are cities with populations of more than 10 million. There are six megacities in North and South America, only one (Cairo) in Africa, two (Istanbul and Moscow) in Europe, and ten in Asia.
3. The eastern part of North America, much of northern Europe, and Southeast Asia have experienced significant deforestation. Desertification or the risk of it is seen most in the Middle East; north, central, and parts of South Africa; the southern part of India; Australia; the northwest section of North America; and the eastern part of South America. Pollution is especially evident on the coastlines and on major shipping routes.
4. The regions most affected by human activity are red on the inset map (Europe, India, Asia, the eastern part of North America, etc.). The least affected are green (Canada, the western part of North America, much of Africa and South America, Australia, etc.).

IDEAS FOR . . . Expansion

Ask students to locate their home country on the maps and tell about the types of human impact that are significant there. Ask: *Why are these things occurring? Do these kinds of impact have an effect on other places?* For example, forest clearing for agriculture and forest fires in Indonesia often spread smoke pollution far beyond the areas where deforestation occurs, especially to Singapore and Malaysia.

Preparing to Read *(pages 4–5)*

30 mins

WARM-UP

Some target vocabulary is presented in a report of a conference about reducing global carbon emissions. Ask: *What are some sources of carbon emissions?* (the combustion of fossil fuels such as coal, natural gas, and oil for energy and transportation) *What do you know about the relationship between global warming and carbon emissions? Do scientists agree about the link? What can people do to reduce carbon emissions?*

Exercise A. | Building Vocabulary

- Have students find the words in blue in the reading and use the other words around them to guess their meanings.

- Remind students that looking at the part of speech can help them figure out the meaning. Clues from surrounding words identify the part of speech. For example, *conference* and *equivalent* are preceded by the article *the*, indicating that the words are nouns. *Eliminate* has the infinitive form *to* and *devoted* is paired with *was*, indicating both are verbs.

- Allow time for students to complete the exercise individually.

Vocabulary Notes

The Qatar conference was *devoted to* or focused exclusively on the topic of climate change. However, the phrase *be devoted to* usually has a more emotional meaning of having strong love for or loyalty to someone. *Marcia, an environmental activist, is devoted to researching ozone layers at work, but when she comes home, she is devoted to her family.*

Word Link

The prefix *equi-* has the sense of equal or equally. Therefore, something that is *equivalent* is basically the same as something else. If a decision is *equitable*, it is fair so that everyone is treated equally. A triangle that is *equilateral* has sides of the same length. Ask what *equidistant* means.

TIP

Ask students for other words that are equivalent to *perspective*. Some possibilities are *point of view, attitude, position, outlook, frame of mind,* and *stand* or *stance*. Ask: *Which of these words could be substituted for* perspective *in the passage about carbon emissions? Which ones are often paired with positive or negative?*

Answer Key

1. ignore
2. equivalent
3. be devoted to
4. conference
5. eliminate
6. perspective

Exercise B. | Building Vocabulary

- Students complete the sentences with words from the box. Encourage them to try to match words with the context before looking words up in a dictionary.

- Compare answers as a class.

Vocabulary Notes

Point out that the plural word *criteria* refers to principles or standards by which you are going to judge something. A *criterion* is one singular factor that you use to decide about something. Other synonyms for *criteria* are *standards, measures,* or *benchmarks*. For example, in many countries the *criteria* for university entrance are good grades at secondary school, recommendations, and a high score on an entrance examination. Typically, all candidates are judged by the same *criteria*.

Answer Key

1. shifting 2. criteria 3. compound 4. register
5. concept 6. incorporate

Exercise C. | Using Vocabulary

- Ask students to think about answers to the questions before talking with a partner about them.

- Ask pairs to share their responses with the class.

Answer Key

Answers will vary. **1.** Students may respond with some of the environmental issues from earlier pages. **2.** Many household cleaning products contain harmful chemical compounds such as chlorine and ammonia. **3.** While most scientists believe that human activities play a large role in global warming, others think warming is part of a natural cycle of temperature change.

IDEAS FOR . . . Expansion

Advise students to start a vocabulary notebook. Demonstrate on the board how to write new words in the notebook. Ask students for suggestions about what information to include. For example, they might include translations, example sentences, or collocations (words that commonly appear together).

Exercise D. | Brainstorming

- Students work in groups of three or four to discuss the questions.
- Bring the class together and ask for suggestions to write on the board.

Answer Key

Possible answers:

The fossil record gives a good idea of plants and animals that existed in the past. We can also tell about changing environments by using ice cores or sediment cores that cover long periods of time.

Exercise E. | Previewing and Predicting

- Ask students to look at the photographs and infographics, or diagrams, on pages 6 through 12, paying special attention to the captions.
- Next, students read the title and the first sentence of each paragraph, noting that the paragraphs are identified by letter.
- Students predict what the passage will contain by choosing answers.
- Note that the infographic on page 10 will be studied in exercise **D** on page 14.
- Check the answers *after* students read the passage.

 track **1-01** You may want to play the audio while students read. Remind students that the vocabulary definitions in the numbered footnotes at the bottom of pages will help them understand the reading.

Overview of the Reading

Some scientists have proposed a new geological epoch called the *Anthropocene* because it reflects human impact on Earth. The passage starts by describing the origins of the idea. Although a similar idea was proposed in the 1870s, the current term has only been in use for about a decade.

Geologists are still deciding whether to adopt the term Anthropocene because they usually wait until changes in stratigraphy are noted before deciding that an epoch has changed. Most of the article is devoted to examining ways human impact might show up in the geological record, focusing on cities, agribusiness, deforestation, and polluting the atmosphere. The conclusion of the passage suggests that renaming might draw attention to the consequences of human actions.

The article by Elizabeth Kolbert originally appeared in *National Geographic* in March 2011 and can be found at http://ngm.nationalgeographic.com/2011/03/age-of-man/kolbert-text

Key Concepts

Review the following key concepts with reference to the infographic on page 8.

Geological Time

Geologists focus on *strata,* or layers of the earth's crust, to understand the environment and living things during the past. There is an assumption that older layers of rock are covered by more recent layers, although sometimes events such as earthquakes or plate movement can disrupt the sequence. Each *stratum,* or layer, has its own special characteristics and often contains fossils of particular kinds of living things. When plants or creatures that were common in an earlier layer disappear or become extinct, it indicates that a great change has taken place, so the next layer of stratigraphy is given a different name or label. These changes are called *boundary events.*

The passage—and especially paragraph F and the chart below it—use special words for different lengths of geological time. *Epoch*—the one at issue in this reading—is the shortest length of time, followed by *period* and *era,* each much longer spans of time.

Scientists are able to use radiometric dating to calculate the absolute age of natural materials because they know the decay rates of radioactive materials found in them.

If you rotate the infographic on page 8 ninety degrees, you'll see the hierarchy of terms with *era* including several *periods* and each period including several *epochs.*

IDEAS FOR... Checking Comprehension

1. *According to the author, what are some of the main ways humans are changing the planet?* (building cities, farming, deforestation, adding CO_2 to the atmosphere)

2. *Which lasting traces of human activity might appear in the rocks eventually?* (plant pollen, sedimentation changes, movement of plants and animals, extinction of species or coral reefs)

IDEAS FOR... Expansion

Ask students to name types of earth scientists. Possibilities are geologists (who study rocks), paleontologists (who study fossils), petrologists (who search for oil), oceanographers (marine scientists), and meteorologists (who study climate and weather). Use the key words *earth science* to find out more about their work.

How do earth scientists use stratigraphy as markers of time? Search the Internet using key words: *geologic time scale*

A short video gives a good introduction at **http://www.natgeoeducationvideo.com/film/1032/the-geologic-time-scale** which can be followed by an interactive time line at **http://science.nationalgeographic.com/science/prehistoric-world/prehistoric-time-line/**

Other helpful websites on geological time include **http://www.ucmp.berkeley.edu/help/timeform.php** and **http://geology.com/time.htm**

⊙ Understanding the Reading
45 mins
(pages 13–15)

Check students' predictions in exercise **E** on page 5.

Answer Key

1. c, geology 2. b, the current period 3. b, the overall human impact

Before proceeding with the comprehension questions, ask the class if there were areas of the reading that they didn't understand. Write the letters of the paragraphs or problematic vocabulary on the board and return to them if they are not clarified in the comprehension activities.

Exercise A. | Identifying Main Ideas

- Ask students to read the questions. If necessary, have them look back at the passage and reread the relevant paragraphs.

- Check the answers as a class and ask students to explain their choices by referring to lettered paragraphs in the text.

NOTE: Throughout this teacher's guide, letters in brackets are used to indicate the paragraph where the answer is found.

Answer Key

1. epoch [F] 2. Answers will vary, but a possibility is: *The Anthropocene is an epoch when humans will leave a clear geological record of their impact on the earth.* 3. [A] Tracing the Origins of the Anthropocene; [H] How We Are Changing the Planet; [N] A New Perspective on Earth's History; 4. cities, agriculture, deforestation, and chemical changes of the atmosphere

Exercise B. | Identifying Key Details

- Allow time for students to write their answers individually.

- After students complete the exercise, check answers as a class. Invite volunteers to say where they found the answers to the items.

Answer Key

1. 1870s, Anthropozoic [C] 2. man-made materials; They will be eroded. [H] 3. Fertilizers contain large amounts of nitrogen, only part of which is used by plants. The rest runs off and creates algae blooms in waterways. Industrial farming concentrates on a limited range of plants instead of the biodiversity that characterized the land in the past. [J] 4. Deforestation increases sedimentation through erosion, and habitat loss leads to the extinction of species. [K] 5. Due to climate change, some plants and animals seek cooler environments. [L] The acidification of the ocean means that coral reefs are dying. [M]

Exercise C. | Critical Thinking: Evaluating

- Students should use information from the preceding exercise to complete the summary chart.

- Then, working in groups of three or four, students discuss what evidence of human activity would be left in the fossil record.

- Compare responses as a class, asking students to support their ideas with references to the reading passage.

Answer Key

1. cities: man-made, erosion [H] **2.** farming: perhaps, pollen [J] **3.** forests: deforestation, extinctions (due to loss of habitat) [K] **4.** atmosphere: polluting/changing, the fossil record, acidification, reef gap [M]

Exercise D. | Understanding Infographics

- Ask students to focus on the infographic on page 10 until they understand its major features. Go over these as a class.

- In this case, there are three variables—population, affluence, and technology—that work together to intensify the amount of human impact.

- World GDP, or Gross Domestic Product, is used to represent affluence, while patent applications stand for technology.

- The diagram shows each of the three components on its own axis in relation to three points in time: 1900, 1950, and 2011. Amounts are given for each date.

- Ask students to answer the questions and then compare their answers with a partner.

- Go over responses as a class, especially the explanations for the I=PAT formula.

Vocabulary Notes

In American English, a *million* has 6 zeros, a *billion* has 9 zeros, and a *trillion* has 12 zeros. However, in British English, *thousand* and *million* are the same, but until recently, a *billion* had 12 zeros and a *trillion* 18 zeros. Now the two systems seem to have settled on the American standard.

Answer Key

1. b **2.** Human impact results from a combination of increases in population, technology, and affluence. **3.** Population grew by 39 percent from 1900 to 1950, then by almost three times to 2011. GDP nearly tripled in the first 50 years, then grew by about 10 times from 1950 to 2011. Technology nearly tripled in the period 1900–1950, then grew by more than four times to 2011. Of the three factors, GDP grew the most.

CT Focus: Analyzing Arguments

- Go over the information in the **CT Focus** box, noting the two steps. First, identify the author's argument, and then analyze the evidence used to support the argument. Think of a checklist for the evidence:

- ☐ Is it developed so that you can follow it?
- ☐ Is it accurate?
- ☐ Is it detailed?
- ☐ Is it current or up-to-date?

- How can you tell if it is accurate? (Look at other sources of information, see what authorities are mentioned.) Look for recent dates to see if the evidence is current.

Exercise E. | Critical Thinking: Analyzing Evidence

- Contentious arguments have several perspectives or ways of interpreting the evidence. Here, the students have to identify and evaluate the evidence presented in the reading.

- Students look for evidence and sort it into the two positions. Then they discuss their findings with a partner.

- As students discuss the evidence, they should consider the criteria listed above.

Answer Key

Arguments For: Other scientists find the concept useful [D, E]; stratigraphers think that human impact will be "stratigraphically significant" [G]; the pollen record will show agricultural focus on a limited range of plants [J]; erosion from deforestation increases the amount of sediment [K]; habitat loss will lead to extinctions that will show up in the fossil record [K]; similarly, the fossil record will show shifts in habitat due to global warming [L]; CO_2 acidifies oceans so that corals cannot form reefs [M]

Arguments Against: Some geologists say we have to wait to see what appears in the stratigraphic record [F]; cities will not survive erosion [H]; scientists can't tell the difference between synthesized and natural nitrogen [J]; dams on rivers are disrupting the natural sedimentation process [K]

1. There is more evidence in support than against. **2.** Answers will vary.

> **TIP** You may want to introduce some language for talking about arguments. For example, the person who supports an idea is a *proponent*. The person who takes the opposite position is an *opponent*. For example, *Proponents of the idea that excess carbon dioxide causes global warming think we ought to control industrial emissions. By contrast, opponents claim that global warming is a natural process and not caused by human activity.*

Exercise F. | Identifying Meaning from Context

- Encourage students to find the words or expressions and guess what they mean in the context of the paragraph. Only then should they return to the page and select the closest match.

- Students might want to create new sentences using these items for their vocabulary notebook.

Answer Key

1. f **2.** c **3.** e **4.** g **5.** b **6.** d **7.** a

Developing Reading Skills
(page 16)

45 mins

Reading Skill: Understanding Cohesion

- Explain that it is important to understand how ideas are linked together in a reading passage. Later, students will use similar cohesive devices in their writing.

- Go over the information in the **Reading Skill** box.

- It is useful to mark up a text with circles, underlines, and arrows to see clearly how words and concepts are related.

Exercise A. | Analyzing

The exercise gives guided practice in identifying referents.

Answer Key

1. b **2.** a

Exercise B. | Analyzing

Students find the referents in paragraphs of the reading passage.

Answer Key

1. Anthropocene **2.** commonly fossilized organism **3.** a change **4.** reef gap

---

IDEAS FOR ... Expansion

Students who want to learn more about the Anthropocene concept can explore it at several sites: **http://www.metanexus.net/blog/anthropocene-and-noosphere** has a 3-minute summary video of the reasons for renaming the epoch.

Listen to an 18-minute TED talk on the Anthropocene at **http://tedxtalks.ted.com/video/TEDxCanberra-Will-Steffen-The-A**

There's a website about the proposed epoch with many links at **http://www.anthropocene.info/en/home**

Viewing: Man-Made Earthquakes *(page 17)*

30 mins

TIP The first few times you use a video in class, you might consider having the students just watch to note the gist of the video the first time, then watch again to focus on answering questions. This is analogous to having students skim a reading passage before reading it thoroughly.

Overview of the Video

A mining town in Australia experienced a serious earthquake that scientists say resulted from the underground network of mining tunnels. The mining activity exacerbated or made worse the pre-existing underground stresses.

Background Note

Movements and stresses in the earth's crust are normal, but some human activities can make them worse and actually trigger an earthquake. Dams that hold back large amounts of water are one cause. Extracting oil, gas, or minerals are other activities that can induce stress. Recently, a process called fracking has resulted in large amounts of water injected into the ground; this is another cause of seismic activity.

Before Viewing

Exercise A. | Using a Dictionary

- Have students work individually to match the words and their definitions.
- Compare the answers as a class.
- Ask students to predict how these words will be used in the video.

Answer Key

1. perturb 2. excavation 3. stress 4. induced 5. extract

Exercise B. | Thinking Ahead

Discuss different kinds of mining. Some valuable minerals that are extracted include coal, gold, diamonds, copper, tin, etc. These materials are worth a lot of money, but miners work in dangerous conditions and often experience poor health. Disasters such as mine collapses are common.

While Viewing

- Suggest that students read the questions so they are prepared to watch and listen for certain information. They should underline the key information in each question.
- As students watch, they take very brief notes, just enough to answer the questions or remind them what the answer was after viewing.
- Allow enough time for students to complete their answers. Ask if anyone needs to watch the video again.

After Viewing

Exercise A.

- Have students work in pairs to discuss and compare answers.
- Ask students if there are any points that are unclear that they wish to discuss.

Answer Key

1. Newcastle, Australia
2. Thirteen people died, 160 were injured, and $4 billion U.S. dollars of damage occurred.
3. The extensive coal mines made the stress worse.
4. Stresses occur in the earth's crust, but earthquakes rebalance the stresses.
5. About 50 percent of human-triggered earthquakes may be caused by mining.

Exercise B. | Critical Thinking: Synthesizing

Answer Key

Mining creates holes in the earth and disturbs layers. In some cases, mining adds fluids underground that create more stress, which in turn can lead to earthquakes.

IDEAS FOR ... **Expansion**

- Ask: *What evidence of mining would geologists see in stratigraphy?* (The natural layers and deposits of minerals such as coal would be disturbed. In the Appalachian area of the United States, coal companies are taking mountains apart to reach seams of coal. The geologist can see exactly what has happened. In a strip mine, such as the one in the photograph on page 17, it is evident that the natural layers of the earth have been cut away artificially to find gold.)

- Lead a brief class discussion on whether humans can substitute other materials for things that are mined or extracted from the earth. For example, instead of using coal to create electrical power, is it possible to use renewable energy such as solar or wind energy?

Exploring Written English
(pages 18–20)

45 mins

- Read aloud the writing goal. Mention that cause-and-effect is a common type of essay.

- Remind students that writing is a process. Just as there are stages of reading or viewing that lead to comprehension, there are stages in the writing process that lead to producing a final draft. The lesson starts with brainstorming, then goes on to a review of language for writing, and then presents the steps in the writing process.

- This is a good opportunity to remind students about the Independent Student Handbook at the back of their Student Book. Pages 246–248 have useful tips on academic writing and research.

Exercise A. | Brainstorming

- Brainstorming is a useful first step for getting ideas before writing. In this case, students think about communities or groups they belong to. What kinds of activities do they do that have some effects other than the intended ones?

- Students should write their ideas in the chart and then share them with a partner.

- Ask: *Did sharing your ideas give you some other suggestions to consider?*

Exercise B. | Vocabulary for Writing

- Have students locate the words in the lettered paragraphs of the main reading and guess their meanings from context before using the words to complete the sentences.

- Check answers as a class, asking students to use each word in a new sentence.

Answer Key

1. traces 2. deplete 3. preserve 4. transform
5. the dominant force 6. The emergence

Free Writing

- Explain that free writing is writing rapidly to come up with ideas without worrying about mistakes.

- Set a time limit of five minutes for students to free write about one activity that has effects. Encourage students to use vocabulary from exercise **B**.

Exercise C.

- Go over the information in the **Language for Writing** box.

- Note that good writers use cohesive devices to avoid repetition.

- Point out that each sentence in the exercise has a clue about the form to use in completing the second sentence.

- Invite volunteers to write their answers on the board, explaining their choice of word.

Answer Key

1. these 2. epoch 3. activities 4. reduction 5. harmful

Exercise D.

Students write six additional sentences using cohesive devices to expand upon their ideas in the free writing section.

Writing Skill: Reviewing Essay Writing

- Have students read the information in the box.

- As a review of essay writing, ask: *What are the three main parts of an essay?* (introduction, body, conclusion) *What is a thesis statement and where does it appear?* (The main idea of the essay occurs in the introduction.) *What should each body paragraph do?* (Each body paragraph should present one main idea, using key words from the thesis statement.) *What should you repeat in the conclusion?* (the thesis statement)

- Ask how the essay prompt should be reflected in the writing.

Exercise E. | Critical Thinking: Evaluating

- Students decide which thesis statement is most appropriate for the essay prompt.

- Discuss what criteria to use. Responses may include the following: using some key words from the prompt, responding with an opinion or position, and keeping on topic.

- Allow time for students to discuss the choices in pairs. Then, ask what criteria led to their choices. Response "b" is best because "a" and "d" are too vague and "c" is off-topic. Response "b" also makes the best use of key words from the prompt.

Exercise F. | Critical Thinking: Evaluating

Given the choice of thesis statement "b" from exercise **E**, students select three ideas for the body paragraphs.

Answer Key

Choices c, d, and e all support the idea of making environmentally friendly food choices, whereas choices a and b are too general and don't support the thesis statement.

Exercise G. | Applying

Students then use their choices from exercise **F** to complete the sentences.

Answer Key

Wording will vary. Possible answers:

One way that we can help heal the planet is to choose food that doesn't contribute to pollution.

Another way we can heal the planet is to choose foods that preserve endangered species.

Finally, we can help heal the planet by selecting foods that use fewer resources such as water.

Exercise H. | Discussion

• Ask the class to brainstorm ways they would like to improve their school. Write several ideas on the board. For each idea, ask for some concrete suggestions for putting that idea into practice. For example, if the idea is reducing the amount of paper used, some suggestions might be having students submit work electronically, having computer-based tests, or using e-books in the library.

• Then work as a group to form a thesis statement such as: *Unnecessary paper consumption causes environmental problems such as cutting down forests and generating trash for landfills. Our college could reduce paper use by making better use of technology. Three ways we could use technology more effectively are having students submit work electronically, using computer-based exams instead of paper exams, and acquiring e-books for the campus library.*

• After working as a class, students work with a partner to develop a thesis statement and three supporting ideas for the body paragraphs.

Writing Task: Drafting

(page 21)

Exercise A. | Planning

• Point out that this planning chart is a useful way to organize ideas before writing.

• Go over the five steps in the exercise.

• Point out that complete sentences are not necessary for the details and notes in the planning chart. The important thing is to get some ideas down on paper.

• Allow time for students to complete their charts, using ideas from exercise **A** and **Free Writing** as appropriate.

• Move around the class while students are writing, offering help and advice as needed.

• Ask one or two students to read their thesis statement aloud to the class.

Exercise B. | Draft 1

Remind the class that the purpose of a first draft is to get ideas down on paper. They will have time to revise and edit later.

Writing Task: Revising

(pages 22–23)

Exercise C. | Critical Thinking: Analyzing

• Explain that analyzing this model essay will help students to revise their own writing.

• Sometimes it is helpful for students to have a visual image of an essay's organization. Suggest that this essay is something like a sandwich with the introductory paragraph and conclusion similar to outside slices of bread. The three body paragraphs are like the filling—meat, fish, eggs, or cheese—the important components that make it a particular kind of sandwich. The supporting details for each main idea are like the salad dressing, mustard, or condiments that add spice and flavor.

Answer Key

1. The first paragraph is the introduction (A), the next three are the body paragraphs (B), and the fifth paragraph is the conclusion (C).
2. The thesis statement is the last sentence in the first paragraph.
3. Key words or concepts include *green spaces*, *mixed-use areas*, and *rooftop gardens*.
4. The topic sentences occur as the first sentences in paragraphs two, three, and four.
5. The key words from the thesis statement are repeated in the topic sentences: green spaces, mixed-use areas, rooftop gardens.

Exercise D. | Revising

Explain that these steps will help students to reread their work carefully and look for ways to improve it.

Exercise E. | Peer Evaluation

• Explain that this process will help students to see if they have organized their ideas clearly. Sometimes students see things in another person's work that they don't see in their own.

- Discuss the four steps in the evaluation process to make sure students know what to do.
- Emphasize that it is really important to start by finding something positive to say.
- Ensure that both members of the pair have equal time to give feedback.

Writing Task: Editing

(page 24)

Exercise F. | Draft 2

Walk around and monitor students as they work. Provide assistance as needed.

Exercise G. | Editing Practice

- Go over the information in the box.
- Allow time for students to find and correct the mistakes.
- Invite volunteers to write the corrected sentences on the board.

Answer Key

1. One reason to limit the use of pesticides is that **they contain** harmful compounds.
2. Some people are installing rooftop gardens and using solar panels in their homes. **These actions** can save money and resources.
3. Many fish species have become extinct and, as a result, there is less biodiversity in our oceans. **This is** a problem because **it upsets** the natural balance of the oceans' ecosystems.

Exercise H. | Editing Checklist

- Read aloud the sentences in the editing checklist.
- Allow time for students to read and edit their work.

Exercise I. | Final Draft

- Some teachers set this task for homework so that all students have the time they need to revise and edit their work.
- Collect students' work.
- Let them know when they can expect to get their essays back. At that time, be sure to go over the marking system that you use.

TIP You may want to suggest that students keep copies of their drafts in a portfolio so that they can see how their writing develops over the course of several drafts.

IDEAS FOR . . . Further Research

Suggest that students keep a topic journal for this course. As they read topics in each unit, have them write down ideas that they would like to explore further. Often, reading about a fascinating topic makes it more salient so that information or news about that topic seems relevant. A topic journal helps students keep track of information that they may make use of in some of their other courses.

Conservation and Protection

Academic Track
Environmental Science/
Life Science

Academic Pathways:
Lesson A: Understanding appositives
          Analyzing text organization
Lesson B: Reviewing the thesis statement
          Writing a persuasive essay

Unit Theme

Unit 2 explores the worldwide decline in the population of big cats with a special focus on tigers. The main reading passage provides an overview of tiger conservation projects today and argues that we must do more to save the species.

 ## Think and Discuss *(page 25)*

5 mins

- Ask students to describe the photo. Ask: *Where is the child and why is he holding a photo of a tiger? What happened to the tiger?* (He is outside a zoo in Indonesia where a tiger has been killed by poachers.)

- Discuss the concept of poaching. *What is a poacher?* (Someone who illegally kills or captures an animal.) *Why would a poacher kill a zoo animal?* (People pay a lot of money for tiger body parts for folk medicine.)

- Discuss possible answers to question 1. Remind students that *species* refers to both plants and animals, although this unit is about animals. Endangered species are at risk of becoming extinct. A number of large cats (Barbary lion, Asian cheetah, Amur leopard, Iberian lynx) are endangered, but so are some birds (condor, Philippine eagle), primates (mountain gorilla, orangutan), and many other animals.

- For question 2, reasons why some animals are endangered might include loss of habitat, hunting or killing the animals, and loss of the animals' food source. Encourage the class to relate these reasons to ideas from Unit 1 such as deforestation, expansion of the human population, and ecological changes such as global warming.

- Discuss the meaning of the unit title and how it might relate to the photo. Most poaching occurs with animals living in the wild, not in zoos that are meant to protect and conserve them.

Exploring the Theme
(pages 26–27)

15 mins

- The opening spread features photographs of eight large cats with information about their distribution, population size, and endangered status.

- Allow time for students to read the information for each animal before they work with a partner to find answers to the questions.

- As pairs of students work together, ask them to compare the big cats, paying special attention to the words that are used for status. Ask them which word means most endangered and which means least at risk. (*Endangered* is at risk of extinction now, *vulnerable* is at risk not long from now, *near threatened* means may be at risk in the future, and *least concern* means there is no immediate threat.)

- Discuss question 2, asking about the place these animals have in nature. For example, what does it mean to be a "top predator"? (It is the animal at the top of the food chain.)

- Discuss question 3. Biologist George Schaller has spent his life studying animal behavior, but especially big cats. He is working on a project in Tibet to create a way for people to co-exist with snow leopards, one of the most endangered species. Schaller is the vice-president of Panthera, a conservation group mentioned in the reading passage.

Answer Key

Possible answers:

1. According to the scale above, the snow leopard and tiger are most endangered.
2. Each type of big cat is a unique species that has a special position at the top of the food chain in its environment.
3. Schaller knows that some big cats are at such risk that if we don't act very soon, they will become extinct. If humans put their own needs first instead of making changes to share the planet with other living things, tigers and other endangered cats will cease to exist.

IDEAS FOR . . . Expansion

National Geographic photographer Vincent Musi took the pictures of cats featured on pages 26 and 27 at the Houston Zoo under special conditions where the cats were just feet away in an enclosure. Sometimes it took up to three days to get the photograph Musi wanted. Have interested students visit **http://ngm.nationalgeographic.com/big-cats#/2** to learn more about the project and see Musi's photographs.

---

30 mins

Preparing to Read
(pages 28–29)

WARM-UP

Some target vocabulary is presented in the context of a re-assessment of strategies for protecting wild animals from extinction.

Ask: *What kinds of conservation programs for wild animals do you know about? Do they work to protect the animals? Give examples of programs that are successful.*

Exercise A. | Building Vocabulary

- Have students find the words in blue in the reading and use the other words around them to guess their meanings.

- Remind students that looking at the part of speech can help them figure out the meaning. Clues from surrounding words identify the part of speech. For example, *hypothetical* modifies the noun *problem,* so it is an adjective. On the other hand, both *authorities* and *priority* are modified by adjectives, so they are nouns. *Assess* has the infinitive form *to* and both *project* and *acknowledge* are used as verbs.

- Allow time for students to complete the exercise individually.

Word Partners

A *priority* is something that is more important than other things, so it must be done first. It comes from the word *prior,* meaning coming before in time or importance. However, the collocation *low priority* indicates that something has a low position on a list, so it can be dealt with after higher priorities.

> **TIP** Some effective managers start every day by prioritizing things they need to do. This strategy works for students too and can help make the best use of limited time. Ask: *What kinds of factors would help students prioritize things they need to do?* Some answers might include assignments that are due, scheduled exams, or important appointments or deadlines.

Answer Key

1. acknowledge
2. Authorities
3. hypothetical
4. priority
5. assess
6. project

Vocabulary Notes

Something that is *hypothetical* is based on a theory or a logical idea, but not something based on reality or actual facts. Hypothetical ideas are part of the process of exploring possibilities, but they need to be tested before they are really useful.

Exercise B. | Building Vocabulary

- Students complete the sentences with words from the box. Encourage them to try matching words using the context before looking words up in a dictionary.

- Compare answers as a class.

Word Partners

Intrinsic nature refers to qualities that are basic or essential to something. Cats, for example, are intrinsically independent.

Answer Key

1. maximum 2. infinite 3. Resolve 4. intrinsic 5. apparently 6. induce

Exercise C. | Using Vocabulary

- Ask students to think about answers to the questions before talking with a partner about them.
- Ask pairs to share their responses with the class.
- Note that *resolve* is often paired with New Year's resolutions when people say what changes they will make in their lives during the coming year.

Answer Key

Answers will vary, but point out that writers often identify authorities by describing their research, accomplishments, or membership in an organization. There are several instances of this in the reading passage.

IDEAS FOR . . . Expansion

When searching for useful articles on the Internet, it is important to know whether the author is considered an authority on the subject. On National Geographic sites, there is typically an identification of the author at the bottom of the reading passage that describes the author's credentials or experience. By contrast, Wikipedia is crowd-sourced, so it is not easy to identify contributors or their expertise.

Exercise D. | Brainstorming

- Students work in groups of three or four to discuss the questions.
- Bring the class together and ask for suggestions to write on the board.

Answer Key

Possible answers:

Some animals have lost their habitat because of human expansion into wild areas or forests. Others are hunted for their skins, tusks, or body parts. Setting aside protected areas where people cannot hunt or otherwise harm animals may conserve endangered species.

Exercise E. | Predicting

- Ask students to skim the reading passage, paying special attention to photos and their captions.
- Students predict what the passage will include about tigers. They list their ideas.
- Check the answers *after* students read the passage.

 track **1-02** You may want to play the audio while students read. Remind students that the vocabulary definitions in the numbered footnotes at the bottom of pages will help them understand the reading.

Overview of the Reading

The author describes the dilemma that tiger conservationists face: They understand the types of habitats that tigers need to thrive and reproduce, but conservation projects to protect tiger populations seem to have failed. Several authorities cited in the passage say that it is still possible to save tigers from extinction, but more effective strategies must be used—and they must be used soon if the species is to continue.

The original article by Caroline Alexander was published in *National Geographic* in December 2011 and can be found at **http://ngm.nationalgeographic.com/2011/12/tigers/alexander-text**

Reading Infographics

Students were asked to look at the photographs as part of previewing the article and predicting its contents. Ask: *How were the close-up photographs of tigers taken?* The photographs on pages 30 and 35 were probably taken with camera traps where the tiger stepped on a device that took the picture with a hidden or camouflaged camera. Ask about the photograph on page 32. *What's wrong with the tiger?* Actually, the animal has been tranquilized with a dart so that researchers can check its health, measure it, and then fit it with a radio collar so that they can track its movements in the wild. Tracking will help identify the tiger's range. This female tiger is pregnant and one researcher is listening to the heartbeat of the fetus.

IDEAS FOR . . . Checking Comprehension

Draw students' attention to the map on page 33. Ask the class to work in groups of three to talk about tiger habitats. Write the following questions on the board and have the students use the map key and inset map to answer them:

1. *What was the historic range of the tiger as contrasted to where tigers are found now?* (Formerly, the range covered Iran and Central Asia, Siberia, and Southeast Asia. The present range is much smaller.)

2. *How would you describe the places where tigers have been seen during the last decade as contrasted to their breeding areas?* (The breeding areas typically are small centers within the larger range.)

3. *Does the map show tigers in all of the protected areas? Why or why not?* (The tigers only appear in a few protected areas, mostly in Thailand, Cambodia, and Indonesia. Perhaps poaching has occurred in other areas or human activity has driven the tigers away.)

4. *Name a place where tigers live close to a densely populated area. What kind of problems could this create?* (Tigers live in Bangladesh's densely populated Sundarbans area where they often attack people, or people kill tigers that have attacked their animals. See the photo on page 34.)

5. *Name three places where tigers could travel on corridors between breeding sites.* (Southwest India, North India and Nepal, and Thailand)

IDEAS FOR . . . Expansion

National Geographic Education has an ongoing project called Big Cats Initiative. At their website there are articles, videos, case studies, maps, and lesson plans. Several of the videos show an expedition to find endangered snow leopards in Afghanistan's Hindu Kush mountains, including setting a camera trap. For more information, see **http://education .nationalgeographic.com/education/collections/ big-cats/?ar_a=1**

Answer Key

Possible ideas are: a description of what tigers are like, reasons why tigers are scarce today, wildlife reserves, tiger conservation programs, and ways to save tigers.

Before proceeding with the comprehension questions, ask the class if there were areas of the reading that they didn't understand. Write the letters of the paragraphs or problematic vocabulary on the board and return to them if they are not clarified in the comprehension activities.

Exercise A. | Identifying Main Ideas

- Ask students to read the questions. If necessary, have them look back at the passage and reread the relevant paragraphs.
- Check the answers as a class and ask students to explain their choices by referring to lettered paragraphs in the text.

NOTE: Throughout this teacher's guide, letters in brackets are used to indicate the paragraph where the answer is found.

Answer Key

1. b [B] **2.** c [E] **3.** c [H] **4.** c [K]

Exercise B. | Scanning for Key Details

- Allow time for students to quickly scan the passage for answers.
- Go over responses as a class, asking in which paragraph the detail was found.

Answer Key

1. e [E] **2.** i [E] **3.** k [F] **4.** b [F] **5.** f [G] **6.** a [M] **7.** l [N] **8.** g [N] **9.** h [N]

Exercise C. | Identifying Reasons and Solutions

- Students use information from the reading to complete the chart.
- Compare responses as a class, asking students to support their ideas with reference to the reading passage.

◯ Understanding the Reading
(pages 36–37)

45 mins

Check students' predictions in exercise **E** on page 29.

Answer Key

Reasons: poverty of people so poaching is a way to earn money, the black market for tiger parts, habitat loss from deforestation Solutions: setting aside corridors between breeding areas, creating sanctuaries where tigers cannot be hunted and patrolling them against poachers, working with local human populations to create eco-developments

CT Focus: Analyzing Text Organization

Go over the information in the **CT Focus** box. Remind students that authors may have several equally effective ways to organize information, but that they consider their audience in deciding which organization to use.

Exercise D. | Critical Thinking: Analyzing Organization

- Students skim the reading passage to identify paragraphs that match the ideas. They write the letter of the paragraph after the statement so they can use alphabetical order for the sequence.

- After students complete the exercise, check answers as a class. Invite volunteers to say where they found the answers to the items.

- Note: It is possible to answer item d by saying the description of corridors starts in paragraph G, followed by reference to the plan in paragraph H.

Answer Key

a. 3 [E] **b.** 5 [J] **c.** 1 [B] **d.** 4 [G-H] **e.** 2 [D]

Exercise E. | Critical Thinking: Evaluating

- Students work with a partner to discuss the questions. Remind students of the vocabulary on page 28 that might be useful in their discussion.

- Ask: *Who is the audience for this piece of writing? Why does it start with a description of tigers and a personal account of seeing a tiger?*

Answer Key

Answers will vary. Possible answers:

1. The reading comes from *National Geographic,* which has a wide readership.
2. People are "drawn in" to the reading by the vivid personal description, even if they don't know much about tiger preservation.
3. Answers may vary, but one suggestion is that the author could have started by discussing the endangered status of tigers, measures that have been tried in the past, then proposing alternative approaches to protecting tiger populations.

Exercise F. | Identifying Meaning from Context

- Encourage students to find the words or expressions and guess what they mean in the context of that paragraph. Only then should they return to the page and select the closest match.

- Students might want to create new sentences using these items for their vocabulary notebook.

Answer Key

1. e **2.** b **3.** d **4.** f **5.** a **6.** g **7.** c

Exercise G. | Critical Thinking: Personalizing

Ask students to take a few moments to think about their response and write it down before working in a small group.

Answer Key

Answers will vary, but one possible reason is that many people have house cats as pets and in general are fond of cats. Other people are familiar with big cats from visits to zoos or watching animal programs on television, so they admire the power and abilities of tigers, lions, leopards, and cheetahs.

45 mins

Developing Reading Skills
(page 38)

Reading Skill: Understanding Appositives

- Explain that writers use appositives to give further information about a subject without being repetitive. In Lesson B students will use appositives in their writing to create a smooth flow of ideas.

- Go over the information in the **Reading Skill** box.

- It is useful to mark up a text with underlines and circles to see clearly how the appositives and the nouns they describe are related.

Exercise A. | Understanding Appositives

The exercise gives guided practice in identifying referents of appositives.

Answer Key

1. noun phrase = tiger reserve, appositive = one of 40 in India; **2.** noun 1 = Tom Kaplan, appositive 1 = co-founder of Panthera; noun 2 = Panthera, appositive 2 = an organization dedicated to big cats; **3.** noun phrase = actual tigers, appositive = here-and-now, flesh-and-blood tigers; **4.** noun phrase = infrastructure projects, appositive = the kind of development that often destroys habitat; **5.** noun = Mahendra Shrestha, appositive = former director of the Save the Tiger Fund; **6.** noun = Eric Dinerstein, appositive = chief scientist and vice president of conservation science of the WWF

Exercise B. | Applying

Students find additional examples of appositives in the reading from Unit 1, noting the paragraph where found.

Answer Key

[A]: noun = Crutzen, appositive = who shared a Nobel Prize for discovering the effects of ozone-depleting compounds; noun = the Holocene, appositive = the epoch that began at the end of the last ice age 11,500 years ago; [E] noun = Jan Zalasiewicz, appositive = a British geologist; [H] noun = cities, appositive = vast stretches of man-made materials; noun = man-made materials, appositive = steel, glass, concrete, and brick; [O] noun = William Ruddiman, appositive = a paleoclimatologist at the University of Virginia; [P] noun = Mark Williams, appositive = a geologist and colleague of Zalasiewicz's at the University of Leicester in England

IDEAS FOR . . . Expansion

Students who want to learn more about the conservation and protection of big cats can explore several sites: **http://animals.nationalgeographic.com/ animals/big-cats/** has a variety of articles about big cats, including some about conflicts between humans and big cats and some about humans living with lions.

Listen to a TED talk by two wildlife researchers and photographers at **http://www.ted.com/talks/ beverly_dereck_joubert_life_lessons_from_big_ cats.html** The talk features rare photographs of a leopard family and lions that hunt in a swamp.

Explore an interactive map of lion populations that compares distributions in 1750 and now at **http://ngm .nationalgeographic.com/2013/08/lion-conservation/ lion-strongholds**

30 mins

Viewing: Tigers in the Snow
(page 39)

Overview of the Video

The video focuses on the rare Siberian tigers that live in the Amur river basin, a cold, wild forest in Russia's Far East and northern China. These tigers require large areas for their home ranges, but they are now endangered by human activities such as logging and poaching.

Background Note

Although Siberian tigers are the largest and most powerful big cats, they are also among the most endangered. By 1940, there were only about 40 tigers in the wild. Today, the adult breeding population numbers over 400 animals distributed over a wide area. The Siberian Tiger Project started in 1992 and outfitted a number of tigers with radio collars (as seen in the photograph on page 32) to understand more about the tigers' behavior.

In addition to tigers in the wild, there are Siberian tigers in zoos. A captive breeding program is trying to prevent the animals from becoming extinct.

Before Viewing

Exercise A. | Using a Dictionary

- Have students work individually to match the words and their definitions.
- Compare the answers as a class.
- Ask students to predict how these words will be used in the video.

Answer Key

1. stronghold 2. dominant 3. food chain

Exercise B. | Thinking Ahead

Students list possible threats to tigers.

Answer Key

Answers will vary. Some ideas include: Climate (Siberian tigers live in forests that are extremely cold, snowy, and dark for many months of the year, but they are well adapted to the climate), poachers, deforestation, and hunting of some of the animals the tigers eat, such as deer.

While Viewing

- Suggest that students read the questions so they are prepared to watch and listen for certain information. They should underline the key information in each question.
- As students watch, they take very brief notes, just enough to answer the questions or remind them what the answer was after viewing.
- Allow enough time for students to complete their answers. Ask if anyone needs to watch the video again.

TIP The first few times you use a video in class, you might consider having the students just watch to note the gist of the video the first time, then watch again to focus on answering questions. This is analogous to having students skim a reading passage before reading it thoroughly.

After Viewing

Exercise A.

- Have students work in pairs to discuss and compare answers.
- Ask students if there are any points that are unclear that they wish to discuss.

Answer Key

1. They live in a more extreme environment.
2. Male territory is about 500 square miles and female territory is about 200 square miles.
3. poaching and logging
4. The decline has slowed down, to some extent because of better patrolling against poachers.

Exercise B. | Critical Thinking: Synthesizing

Siberian tigers live in a forested area with a less dense human population than tigers in other places, so perhaps there are fewer conflicts between humans and tigers. Furthermore, corridors between breeding areas are available in this sparsely settled area.

Exploring Written English

45 mins

(page 40–42)

- Read aloud the writing goal. Persuasive essays present a solution to a problem in a convincing way.

- Remind students that writing is a process. Just as there are stages of reading or viewing that lead to comprehension, there are stages in the writing process that lead to producing a final draft. The lesson starts with brainstorming, then goes on to a review of language for writing, and then presents the steps in the writing process.

- Remind students about the Independent Student Handbook at the back of their Student Book. Pages 246–248 have useful tips on academic writing and research.

Exercise A. | Brainstorming

- Brainstorming is a useful first step for getting ideas before writing. In this case, students think about animals, buildings, or natural places that people are trying to protect.

- Students should write their ideas before searching online for other suggestions. Using "endangered" as one of the key words will produce good results.

Exercise B. | Vocabulary for Writing

- Have students locate the words in the lettered paragraphs of the main reading and guess their meanings from context before using the words to complete the sentences.

- Check answers as a class, asking students to use each word in a new sentence.

Answer Key

1. grant, funding 2. program 3. objective
4. exacerbates 5. initiative 6. strategy 7. relentless
8. sacrifice

Free Writing

- Explain that free writing is writing rapidly to come up with ideas without worrying about mistakes.

- Set a time limit of five minutes for students to free write about one animal, building, or place that needs protection. Encourage students to use vocabulary from exercise **B**.

Exercise C.

- Go over the information in the **Language for Writing** box.

- Good writers use appositives to avoid repetition and short, choppy sentences.

- Invite volunteers to write their answers on the board, explaining how the appositive works in the sentence.

Answer Key

Note: Wording may differ somewhat as there are several equally valid ways to combine the sentences.
1. The Bengal tiger, one of India's most popular attractions, is its national animal.
2. In addition to tigers, other animals—monkeys, deer, wild boar, owls, and parakeets—live in Ranthambore.
3. Ranthambore, a former private hunting estate, is home to 41 tigers.
4. Fateh Singh Rathore, now the assistant field director of Ranthambore, used to work there when it was a hunting estate.
5. Zaw Win Khaing, the head ranger of a tiger reserve in Myanmar, saw a tiger in 2002.

Writing Skill: Reviewing the Thesis Statement

- Have students read the information in the box.

- As a review of the thesis statement for a persuasive essay, ask the class for things to write on the board as a checklist:

  ❑ It expresses an opinion or position

  ❑ It supports the opinion with reasons

  ❑ It expresses only ideas that are explained in the body paragraphs

  ❑ It contains key words that will link the topic sentences to the thesis statement

Exercise D. | Critical Thinking: Evaluating

- Allow time for students to discuss the choices in pairs. Then, ask what criteria led to their choices. For the first pair, "a" is superior because it meets the criteria identified above. You can see exactly what the topics of the three body paragraphs will be and how they support the writer's opinion.

- For the second pair, "a" provides reasons why the library should be preserved whereas "b" presents an unsupported opinion.

Exercise E. | Critical Thinking: Evaluating

- Students write a thesis statement that gives their opinion and two supporting reasons.

- Note that if students believe governments <u>should</u> support tiger conservation, they defend their reasoning by stating two positive results of this support.

Writing Task: Drafting
(page 43)

Exercise A. | Planning

- Point out that this planning chart is a useful way to organize ideas before writing.

- Go over the two steps in the exercise.

- Note that two reasons are provided: why the place or animal is valuable and why it is currently in danger.

- Point out that complete sentences are not necessary for the details and notes in the planning chart. The important thing is to get some ideas down on paper.

- Allow time for students to complete their charts, using ideas from exercise **A** and **Free Writing** as appropriate.

- Circulate in the class while students are writing, offering help and advice as needed.

- Ask one or two students to read their thesis statement aloud to the class.

Exercise B. | Draft 1

Remind the class that the purpose of a first draft is to get ideas down on paper. They will have time to revise and edit later.

Writing Task: Revising
(pages 44–45)

Exercise C. | Critical Thinking: Analyzing

- Explain that analyzing this model essay will help students to revise their own writing.

- Draw attention to the opening paragraph and the way in which it sets the scene for the rest of the essay by providing important information about Borneo. By the time the thesis statement appears, the reader already understands some of the key issues.

- The two body paragraphs explain the benefits of biodiversity and the rain forest.

- The projects mentioned in the final paragraph detail how they would achieve the goals mentioned in the body paragraphs.

1. The thesis statement is the last sentence in the first paragraph.
2. Key words or concepts include *protect Borneo, home to so many different species, rainforest, reverse damage from climate change*
3. The topic sentences occur as the first sentences in paragraphs two and three. The order of the body paragraphs reflects the order of the thesis statement.
4. Generally, the key words from the thesis statement are repeated in the topic sentences. However, some synonyms are used such as *different forms of life* instead of *so many different species*, and *protect the globe from climate change* instead of *reverse damage from climate change.*
5. In paragraph two, the supporting details include the fact that some species are only found on Borneo and that scientists continue to find new species. For paragraph three, supporting details are that rainforests absorb carbon dioxide and create more oxygen, and that the forests help to create rain.

Exercise D. | Revising

Explain that the five steps in exercise **C** will help students to reread their work carefully and look for ways to improve it.

Exercise E. | Peer Evaluation

- Although students went through this process in the first unit, make sure that they understand what their roles are in the four steps.

- As you circulate through the room, listen for how students present their first comment. If necessary, point out that this should be positive.

- Ensure that both members of the pair have equal time to give feedback.

Writing Task: Editing
(page 46)

Exercise F. | Draft 2

Walk around and monitor students as they work. Provide assistance as needed.

Exercise G. | Editing Practice

- Go over the information in the box.

- Allow time for students to find and correct the mistakes.

- Invite volunteers to write the corrected sentences on the board.

Answer Key

1. Tigers, an endangered species, live throughout Asia.
2. Ranthambore, a tiger reserve, is in India.
3. Tiger conservationists—people who protect tigers—are looking for new solutions.
4. Corridors, paths for safe travel, may help tigers survive in wild areas.
5. There are fewer than 4,000 tigers, the biggest cats in the world.

Exercise H. | Editing Checklist

- Read aloud the sentences in the editing checklist.
- Allow time for students to read and edit their work.

Exercise I. | Final Draft

- Some teachers set this task for homework so that all students have the time they need to revise and edit their work.
- Collect students' work.

- Let the class know when they can expect to get their essays back. At that time, be sure to go over the marking system that you use.

IDEAS FOR . . . Further Research

Ask students to reflect on the unit and see if they have unanswered questions about any of the topics. If so, make a space on the board or notice board where individuals can post questions and try to elicit comments from other class members. These may include websites that they have found useful or suggested key words for searches.

Beautiful

Academic Track
Sociology/Aesthetics

Academic Pathways:

Lesson A: Using a concept map to
identify supporting details
Applying ideas

Lesson B: Supporting a thesis
Writing an evaluative essay

Unit Theme

Unit 3 explores aesthetics, the principles that underlie concepts of beauty in the arts or in nature. In particular, the main reading defines six elements that characterize great photographs.

Think and Discuss *(page 47)*

5 mins

- Ask students to describe the photo. Ask: *What do you see in the photo? What activity is going on here? How has a photograph captured this moment?*

- The photograph magnifies a natural scene in which two ladybugs are drinking water. It just happens that the drops of water reflect flowers, giving the scene an unreal quality.

- Discuss possible answers to questions 1 and 2. The questions are subjective, so individual responses may differ. As students respond, write ideas on the board. Later, go through the items and categorize them as natural or man-made or some combination of both. For example, a rainbow occurs in nature, but a photograph of it means that someone had to think of how to compose it and the best moment to press the shutter.

- Discuss the meaning of the unit title and how it might relate to the photo. Do students find the photograph beautiful? Why or why not?

Exploring the Theme

15 mins

(pages 48–49)

- The opening spread shows statues and fountains outside the Peterhof Palace in St. Petersburg, Russia.

- The Peterhof Palace was built in the 1720s when the Russian ruler Peter the Great was determined to create a city and surroundings that rivaled European cultural centers. For example, many features of the Peterhof Palace resemble the French King Louis XIV's palace at Versailles. Today Peterhof Palace is a UNESCO World Heritage Site because the art and architecture capture the European sense of beauty of the 1700s.

- Allow time for students to study the photograph and read the text on the right before asking them to work with a partner to answer the questions.

- In discussing question 2, ask: *Are ideas of beauty the same in all countries? Are ideas of beauty the same over time?* As examples, start a discussion of how fashions change in relatively short periods of time. Ask the class to describe fashions that were popular in the past that would seem strange now.

- For question 3, focus on the statues in the foreground of the photograph. Ask: *Are the bodies realistic or stylized? Do real people look like this? By today's standards, are these individuals attractive?*

- Ask about the building. *Does the design have simple, clean lines, or is it elaborate? Are the architectural features balanced or asymmetrical? Would you like the building more or less if it were a different color?*

Answer Key

Possible answers:

1. Aesthetics is a branch of philosophy that deals with the creation and appreciation of beautiful things.
2. Aesthetic ideas differ from culture to culture and over time. It is possible to look at a work of art from long ago and appreciate it according to the aesthetic values of when and where it was created.
3. Answers will vary according to personal opinions, but some students may admire the way all of the features of the Peterhof fit together. For example, the yellow color of the paint picks up the gold of the statues, and the fountains seem like water statues.

IDEAS FOR . . . Expansion

Ask students to find a picture of a statue that they admire and bring it to class to explain the features that they find attractive.

Students can learn more about the Peterhof Palace by visiting the English website at **http://www .peterhofmuseum.ru/?lang=eng** Photographs of the inside of the palace show the elaborate, golden decorations and paintings for which it is famous.

---

30 mins

Preparing to Read
(pages 50–51)

WARM-UP

Some target vocabulary is presented in a reading about Asian influences on Western artists in the 1800s. Ask students if they are familiar with artists such as van Gogh and Whistler (two painters who worked primarily in oil paints). *What is a woodblock?* (a carved piece of wood from which prints can be made)

Exercise A. | Building Vocabulary

- Have students find the words in blue in the reading and use the other words around them to guess their meanings.

- Remind students that looking at the part of speech can help them figure out the meaning. Clues from surrounding words identify the part of speech. For example, *context* and *notions* are both modified with adjectives, indicating that the words are nouns. *Pursue* has the infinitive form *to,* and *exposed to* and *violated* both occur with past tense endings, indicating all are verbs.

- Draw students' attention to the collocations in the target vocabulary: *insight into, be exposed to, notions of,* and *context of.*

Vocabulary Notes

Students encountered the word *perspective* in Unit 1 where it had the meaning of point of view. Here it is used in an artistic sense to mean creating a feeling of depth or distance on a two-dimensional surface such as paper or a drawing canvas. This includes making distant objects smaller than closer ones and having a "vanishing point" where all the background lines seem to come together. The word *notion* has several meanings. As used in exercise **A** it means an idea, belief, or opinion. As such, notions of beauty can change over time. Another meaning of *notion* is a sudden impulse, often quite fanciful. *Sarah's boyfriend was embarrassed when she had a sudden notion to surprise him with a birthday cake at work!* The third sense of *notion* refers to small household items such as needles and thread.

Answer Key

1. pursue
2. (be) exposed to
3. crucial
4. context
5. insight
6. violated
7. notions

Exercise B. | Building Vocabulary

- Students complete the sentences with words from the box. Encourage them to try to match words with the context before looking words up in a dictionary.

- Compare answers as a class.

Word Partners

Proportion has several different shades of meaning. Several of the word partners in the box use *proportion* to mean an amount in relationship to the whole of something. For example, *the proportion of the population* refers to a section of the entire population that is different or special. In an artistic sense, proportion refers to balance and how things fit together. If the statues at Peterhof were three times as large as they are, they would be *out of proportion* with their context.

Answer Key

1. Depression 2. proportions 3. in the abstract
4. Ethics 5. confer

Exercise C. | Using Vocabulary

- Ask students to think about answers to the questions before talking with a partner about them.
- Ask pairs to share their responses with the class.

Answer Key

Answers will vary. 1. Students may respond to the first question with examples that are considered "great art" in their culture. In North America, art classes refer to famous European works as well as national art. 2. The historical context may be at a time of exploration (paintings of newly discovered natural scenery), changes in politics (portraits or sculptures of important leaders), or of historical events (famous battle scenes). 3. Suggest that students bring a photo of art they admire to share with the class.

IDEAS FOR . . . Expansion

As a class, think of many different types of art and write the names on the board. In this unit so far, students have been exposed to photographs, sculpture, architecture, paintings, and woodblock prints. Other types include pottery, carving, fabric printing, calligraphy, weaving, metallurgy, frescoes, and many other forms. Suggest that students have an exhibit of art from their cultures in the classroom. Photos should have captions that explain the type of art and where and when it was created.

Exercise D. | Brainstorming

- Draw students' attention to the photograph of carrots on page 58. What are the students' reactions to this photograph?
- Students work in groups of three or four to discuss the question.
- Bring the class together and ask for opinions, supported by examples.

Answer Key

Possible answers:

There is a whole area of practical art that deals with objects that are meant for daily use—pottery, furniture, gates, signs, etc.—that are carefully designed to be aesthetically pleasing as well as functional. In addition, many plants are also beautiful and have been admired by artists.

Exercise E. | Predicting

- Have students look at the photographs and read the captions on pages 52–58.
- Have students read the first sentence of each paragraph, noting that the paragraphs are identified by letter.
- Students predict what aspects or features of photography the passage will cover.
- Check the answers *after* students read the passage.

 track **1-03** You may want to play the audio while students read. Remind students that the vocabulary definitions in the numbered footnotes at the bottom of the pages will help them understand the reading.

Overview of the Reading

National Geographic photographer Annie Griffiths argues that all great photographs contain outstanding use of light, composition, moment, palette, time, and wonder. The photographs in the passage were carefully selected to exemplify her points.

Annie Griffiths was one of the first women photographers hired by National Geographic. The reading comes from a photography book she edited called *Simply Beautiful Photographs*. The volume contains photographs from National Geographic's archive or collection of photographs taken in the last century. The photos cover a full range of National Geographic's topics such as exploration, wildlife, cultures, science, and nature. The examples in each chapter illustrate the six principles Griffiths describes in the reading passage.

Griffiths also discusses these six principles in a video that includes other National Geographic photographers talking about creating their photographs. See it at **http://video.nationalgeographic.com/video/photography/photographers/simply-beautiful/**

Key Concepts

Professional photographers agree on some elements of design but disagree on others. For example, some say the major elements that make an outstanding photograph are *line, shape, form, texture, pattern,* and *color. Line* is what makes the viewer see the main point of the photograph and understand how it is organized. In the Peterhof photograph on pages 48 and 49, there is a strong sense of vertical line in the fountains and statues, but this is balanced by the horizontal lines of the palace in the background. *Texture* is whether things appear to be rough or smooth; often the focal point of the photograph stands out by appearing to be sharp or rough against a smooth background.

To learn more about the most important aspects of photographs, use *elements of photography* as search key words.

> ### IDEAS FOR ... Checking Comprehension
>
> Ask students the following question about the reading, or write it on the board.
>
> *You looked at the photographs when you previewed the reading passage. Now that you have read Griffiths' analysis of the pictures, do you see them differently? Explain your answer.*

> ### IDEAS FOR ... Expansion
>
> National Geographic is known for its outstanding photographs. A large section of its website focuses on photography. For homework, ask students to explore the site, **http://photography.nationalgeographic.com/photography/** including the following features:
>
> > Photo of the Day
> > Photo Tips
> > Photographers
>
> Have them make note of one feature from the site that particularly interests them and report on it in the next class.

 # Understanding the Reading

45 mins

(pages 59–60)

Check students' predictions in exercise **E** on page 51.

Answer Key

light, composition, moment, palette, time, and wonder

Before proceeding with the comprehension questions, ask the class if there were areas of the reading that they didn't understand. Write the letters of the paragraphs or problematic vocabulary on the board and return to them if they are not clarified in the comprehension activities.

Exercise A. | Identifying Main Ideas

- Ask students to read the questions. If necessary, have them look back at the passage and reread the relevant paragraphs.
- Check the answers as a class and ask students to explain their choices by referring to lettered paragraphs in the text.

NOTE: Throughout this teacher's guide, letters in brackets are used to indicate the paragraph where the answer is found.

Exercise B. | Identifying Key Details

- Allow time for students to write their answers individually.

- After students complete the exercise, check answers as a class. Invite volunteers to say where they found the answers to the items.

CT Focus: Applying Ideas

Go over the information in the **CT Focus** box. The approach is to test ideas from a reading by applying them to a different context. In this case, the ways to analyze photographs are applied to other photos in the student book.

Exercise C. | Critical Thinking: Applying Ideas

- Students reread the three quotes from paragraph J of the passage.

- Then, working with a partner, students discuss what the quotes mean, giving examples from this unit or the previous ones.

- Compare responses as a class, asking students to support their ideas with examples.

Exercise D. | Identifying Meaning from Context

- Encourage students to find the words or expressions and guess what they mean in the context of the lettered paragraph. Only then should they return to the page and complete the sentences.

- Students might want to create new sentences using these items for their vocabulary notebook.

Exercise E. | Critical Thinking: Reflecting

- The goal of the exercise is for students to think about the impact the reading has had on their own life. In this case, students consider their own attitude toward photography. Ask: *Until now, have you just taken photographs without much regard for light, composition, colors, or the special moment that is captured?*

- It may be helpful if students think about the circumstances in which they take photographs and the equipment they use. For example, pictures taken suddenly with a cell phone may capture some human actions or moods, but probably they are not carefully composed or taken with regard to lighting.

Answer Key

TIP There's a big difference between "point-and-shoot cameras" where the camera automatically figures out settings and more complicated single lens reflex cameras where the photographer can consciously control all the aspects of the photo. Most cell phone cameras and many compact digital models are point-and-shoot cameras. Ask students who have photography as a hobby to explain some of the differences found in professional cameras such as lenses, exposure, shutter speed, etc.

Developing Reading Skills *(page 61)*

45 mins

Reading Skill: Using a Concept Map to Identify Supporting Details

Concept maps are a tool that visually represents ideas and their relationships. In this case, the reader creates a diagram to show how the main ideas are supported by details. At the back of this teacher's guide are graphic organizers for each unit.

Exercise A. | Using a Concept Map

- Find the three main points in paragraphs B through E (the first one is done as an example).

- Briefly define the element and give an example from the photos in the passage.

Answer Key

2. composition: what is included in a photo and how it is arranged, the proportions of things; example: Stanfield's *Girl at the Louvre* [J] **3.** moment: the point at which the photo is taken; example: the Stanfield photo again, with the girl jumping [E]

Exercise B. | Applying

Repeat the process for the next three points in Paragraphs F through I.

Answer Key

1. palette: the range of colors used; example: Kers' *Road with Flowers* [G] **2.** time: the length of exposure (quick or over time); example: Griffiths' Badlands photo [H] **3.** wonder: a new way of seeing; example: Badlands or carrot photo [I]

IDEAS FOR . . . Expansion

As a way of linking Units 2 and 3, students can explore a lengthy interview with wildlife photographer Nick Nichols about his field experience with lions. The reading and associated video links describe the variety of equipment and photographic strategies he used to get photographs of lions in their natural habitat and social groups.

http://news.nationalgeographic.com/ news/2013/08/130802-nick-nichols-lion-photos-infrared-drones-mikrokopter-lion-car/

---

30 mins

Viewing: Oregon Coast
(page 62)

Overview of the Video

American counterculture hero Ken Kesey talks to National Geographic about the coast of Oregon. He is awed by the power of nature as waves crash on the rocky coast. Kesey says that everyone who comes there experiences a sense of being humbled by nature and starts to think strange thoughts.

Background Note

During the 1960s in the United States, a young generation wanted to change society with regard to the war in Vietnam, race relations, gender roles, sexual freedom, and how people dealt with authority. Writer Ken Kesey was a leader in the counterculture movement. He and other writers and intellectuals believed that psychedelic drugs gave them a different perception of reality. Kesey and a group of writers called the Merry Pranksters drove a multicolored bus across America to promote their perspective. Members of the counterculture movement used language in a special way. For example, they said that people who thought the way they did were on the same *wavelength*. In this context, wavelength has nothing to do with ocean waves!

Before Viewing

Exercise A. | Using a Dictionary

- Have students work individually to match the words and their definitions.
- Compare the answers as a class.
- Ask students to predict how these words will be used in the video.

Vocabulary Notes

Several of these words are extreme compared to their synonyms. *Treacherous* is more than just dangerous. Saying that the ocean is treacherous means that it cannot be trusted, that even if it seems calm enough for swimming, powerful currents would sweep you out to sea. Similarly, something that is *theatrical* is exaggerated and dramatic in order to draw attention.

Answer Key

1. treacherous 2. humbling 3. theatrical 4. wavelength
5. counterculture

Exercise B. | Thinking Ahead

Beaches and coastline can vary enormously from gentle, calm sands with shallow water to rocky coasts with violent seas. Ask which kinds of coastline members of the class are familiar with because that has a bearing on emotional reactions. Furthermore, some coasts are subject to radical changes in nature as storms such as hurricanes, typhoons, or tsunamis occur.

While Viewing

- Suggest that students read the questions so they are prepared to watch and listen for certain information. They should underline the key information in each question.
- As students watch, they take very brief notes, just enough to answer the questions or remind them what the answer was after viewing.
- Allow enough time for students to complete their answers. Ask if anyone needs to watch the video again.

> **TIP** In most videos, the soundtrack contains important information, but in this case, the visual images are very significant. Consider playing the video again with the sound turned off so that students can concentrate on what they see.

After Viewing

Exercise A.

- Have students work in pairs to discuss and compare answers.
- Ask students if there are any points that are unclear that they wish to discuss.

Answer Key

Answers will vary. Possible answers:

1. It is implied that he was an author (having written *One Flew Over the Cuckoo's Nest*), but he is identified as a counterculture hero or leader.
2. Kesey is spellbound by the coast, very much under its influence, and it makes him think of strange and magical things.
3. The ocean is so powerful here that it makes people feel small and powerless by contrast.
4. Some words might be wild, violent, unspoiled by development, dramatic.

Exercise B. | Critical Thinking: Synthesizing

A photographer might want to wait for just the right *moment* to catch the waves breaking or the *light* reflecting off the clouds in the sky. The *palette* certainly changes during the day (*time*) and with the presence of clouds. There are many possible ways to *compose* a photograph, and just the coastline itself inspires *wonder*, so all six elements are present.

Exploring Written English
(pages 63–66)

45 mins

- Read aloud the writing goal. Writing about a visual art form is a type of description based on aesthetic criteria.

- Remind students that writing is a process. Just as there are stages of reading or viewing that lead to comprehension, there are stages in the writing process that lead to producing a final draft. The lesson starts with brainstorming, then goes on to a review of language for writing, and then presents the steps in the writing process.

- Remind students about the Independent Student Handbook at the back of their Student Book. Pages 246–248 have useful tips on academic writing and research.

Exercise A. | Brainstorming

- Brainstorming is a useful first step for getting ideas before writing. In this case, students work in pairs to think of examples of visual art (as contrasted to music, dance, poetry, etc.).

- Once a pair has several examples, they should consider the *criteria* or standards to use to judge or evaluate it. Recall that *criteria* was a vocabulary item from Unit 1 and that in the Griffiths article she defines six criteria for judging photographs. Different criteria might be appropriate for sculpture or paintings.

- Ask: *What do you think makes something aesthetically pleasing?*

Exercise B. | Vocabulary for Writing

- Have students locate the words in the lettered paragraphs of the main reading and guess their meanings from context before using the words to complete the sentences.

- Check answers as a class, asking students to use each word in a new sentence.

Answer Key

1. atmospheric 2. aesthetically pleasing 3. within the frame 4. illuminate 5. gradation 6. geometric 7. Pastels

Free Writing

- Remind students that free writing is writing rapidly to come up with ideas without worrying about mistakes.

- Set a time limit of five minutes for students to free write about one work of visual art. Encourage students to use vocabulary from exercise **B**.

Exercise C.

- Go over the information in the **Language for Writing** box.

- Adjective clauses give additional information about a noun. When the information is essential (a restricted adjective clause), commas are not used. By contrast, use commas before *which, who,* or *whose* when they are followed by nonessential information.

- When in doubt, students should read the sentence without the adjective clause to see if it makes sense. If it does, the clause is nonessential, so punctuation is needed.

- The exercise gives practice in creating nonrestrictive clauses.

- There is a special reference section on restrictive and nonrestrictive adjective clauses in the Independent Student Handbook on page 249.

Answer Key

Note: There are several ways to combine the sentences, but here are some possibilities. **1.** The work of Vivian Maier, who was an amateur photographer, was discovered after her death. **2.** Ansel Adams, who was most known for his images of the California wilderness, was an American photographer. **3.** Fallingwater, which was designed as a country retreat, was built for a wealthy family who owned a department store in Pittsburg, USA. **4.** Vincent van Gogh, who was influenced by Japanese art, made a copy of Hiroshige's print *Sudden Shower Over Ohashi Bridge*.

Exercise D.

Students return to their free writing and add nonrestrictive clauses to some sentences. Ask: *What additional information can you think of to make the description more interesting?*

Writing Skill: Supporting a Thesis

- Have students read the information in the box.

- Emphasize that the thesis statement is the unifying element in an essay. It states the main ideas and the order in which they will be developed in body paragraphs, but each of these paragraphs must include additional details and examples to develop the key concepts.

Exercise E. | Critical Thinking: Analyzing

Students test the idea of the thesis statement as the unifying element by predicting the number of body paragraphs and the key concepts that will appear in each topic sentence.

Answer Key

1. There will be two body paragraphs. **2./3.** The first body paragraph will be about the integration of Fallingwater into its natural environment. The second body paragraph will focus on the materials used in the construction of the house. Both topic sentences will state that the features contribute to organic architecture.

Exercise F. | Supporting a Thesis

This section confirms the topic sentences for the two body paragraphs.

Exercise G. | Applying

Students decide whether the details are more appropriate for paragraph 1 or 2.

Answer Key

a. 1 **b.** 1 **c.** 2 **d.** 2 **e.** 1 **f.** 2

Writing Task: Drafting
(page 67)

> **IDEAS FOR . . .** Preliminary Research
>
> **Note:** Students may need advance notice to locate a work of art to analyze. Prior to the class in which they start writing, brainstorm about resources they could use to find artwork to use. These resources might include famous museum sites online—these often have photographs of paintings or sculpture in their collections—or using key words such as *famous buildings* or *online exhibits.* Alternatively, students could focus on an artist they admire and look for works by that person. For example, if a person admires the Impressionist painter Monet, they can search for paintings under that name.
>
> Some museum sites to explore are as follows:
>
> The Hermitage in Saint Petersburg **http://www .hermitagemuseum.org/html_En/08/hm88_0.html**
>
> The British Museum
>
> **http://www.britishmuseum.org/explore.aspx**
>
> The Museum of Modern Art in New York
>
> **http://www.moma.org/explore/multimedia/ interactives/57/interactives-online-projects**
>
> The Louvre in Paris
>
> **http://www.louvre.fr/en**

Exercise A. | Planning

- Point out that this planning chart is a useful way to organize ideas before writing.
- Go over the six steps in the exercise, noting that there will be three body paragraphs, one for each criterion.
- Point out that complete sentences are not necessary for the details and notes in the planning chart. The important thing is to get some ideas down on paper.
- Allow time for students to complete their charts, using ideas from exercise **A** and **Free Writing** as appropriate.
- Move around the class while students are writing, offering help and advice as needed.
- Ask one or two students to read their thesis statement aloud to the class.

Exercise B. | Draft 1

Remind students that the purpose of a first draft is to get ideas down on paper. They will have time to revise and edit later.

Writing Task: Revising
(pages 68–69)

Exercise C. | Critical Thinking: Analyzing

- Explain that analyzing this model essay will help students to revise their own writing.
- Point out how the organization of this essay creates a logical flow so that one idea emerges from another.
- In the introduction, the author engages the reader by asking a question, and then cites two well-known architectural examples. Next, an authority is mentioned as the source for two other important architectural features. These are repeated in the thesis statement, the final sentence in the first paragraph.
- The author effectively makes the point about durability by discussing the features of granite. A different aspect of durability—sustainability—is developed at the end of the first body paragraph.
- The second body paragraph gives many details that support the idea of functionality, in terms of design and accessibility.
- In the third body paragraph, the author develops the notion of beauty with the use of vocabulary that invokes color and shape so the reader can visualize the features of the building.
- The concluding paragraph summarizes the key concepts but also adds a final thought about "peace of mind" that leaves the reader satisfied.

Answer Key

Step 1. The thesis statement is the last sentence in the first paragraph.
Step 2. The key words are *durable, functional,* and *aesthetically pleasing.*
Step 3. The order of ideas in the thesis statement is followed in the body paragraphs. In the first and second body paragraphs, the topic sentence—in each case containing a nonrestrictive adjective clause—is the first sentence of the paragraph. In the third body paragraph, the topic sentence is second, following a sentence that equates beauty with being aesthetically pleasing.
Step 4. The key words from the thesis statement—durable, functional, and aesthetically pleasing—are repeated in the topic sentences.
Step 5. Some examples include the following: **durability:** granite material that is unaffected by pollution and resistant to earthquakes; sustainability with solar energy and cooling gardens; **functionality:** open design with no interior walls and windows for natural light; accessible with entrance at street level and no stairs there; **aesthetically pleasing:** contrast of copper window frames with granite, garden growth flowing on building sides

Exercise D. | Revising

Explain that these steps will help students to reread their work carefully and look for ways to improve it.

Exercise E. | Peer Evaluation

- Remind students that this process will help students to see if they have organized their ideas clearly.
- Ensure that both members of the pair have equal time to give feedback.

Writing Task: Editing

(page 70)

Exercise F. | Draft 2

Walk around and monitor students as they work. Provide assistance as needed.

Exercise G. | Editing Practice

The information in the box focuses on two points, punctuation and the use of *which* instead of *that* to refer to objects in nonrestrictive adjective clauses.

Answer Key

1. This image is an excellent example of composition, which is the way objects are arranged in a photograph.
2. That photograph, which I like best of all, is Berenice Abbott's *Pennsylvania Station.*
3. Another important element is light, which illuminates the objects in a photograph.
4. Moment, which captures time in a photograph, helps to tell the image's story.

Exercise H. | Editing Checklist

- Read aloud the sentences in the editing checklist.
- Allow time for students to read and edit their work.

Exercise I. | Final Draft

- Allow time for students to work on their final draft (or set this for homework).
- Collect students' work.
- Let them know when they can expect to get their essays back. At that time, be sure to go over the marking system that you use.

IDEAS FOR . . . Further Research

Credits for photographs in the Student Book are given on page xvi. For all contributors followed by the initials NGC, further information about the photographers and their work is available at **http://photography.nationalgeographic.com/photography/photographers/**

Powering Our Planet

Academic Track
Interdisciplinary

Academic Pathways:
Lesson A: Recognizing a writer's tone
Interpreting figurative language
Lesson B: Avoiding plagiarism
Writing a summary essay

Unit Theme

Unit 4 explores global changes in energy production and consumption. The main reading passage argues that we are already at a crisis point with global warming and peak oil, so we urgently need to make changes in the type and amount of energy we consume to reduce the amount of CO_2 from fossil fuels.

Think and Discuss *(page 71)*

5 mins

- Ask students to describe the photo. Ask: *Why is some of the traffic moving while the rest of it seems stopped?* (The moving traffic occurs in HOV—high occupancy vehicle—lanes while cars containing only one person are stuck in a traffic jam.)

- Discuss the concept of commuting in urban areas. Ask: *What are the main options for getting to work?* (private vehicles vs. public transportation such as buses, trains, underground railways) *Why do people choose to drive to work instead of taking public transport?* (If you have your own car, you can travel on your schedule and not be dependent on mass transit schedules or routes.) *Are there other transport options?* (It depends upon the place. For example, in Copenhagen, Denmark, a third of commuters ride bicycles to work, some on cycle superhighways just for bikes.)

- Brainstorm possible answers to question 1 and write responses on the board. Students may quickly think of things that obviously use energy, but probe into things that are more subtle. For example, many devices are battery-operated, but the batteries need to be recharged or replaced when they run down.

- One way of clarifying everyday energy use is to think of what happens when there is a power outage due to a storm or accident. Ask: *How do you cook, keep warm, and get news when there is no electricity?* (Note: A generator is simply a way of producing power yourself instead of relying on a grid.)

- Question 2 gets at two sources. First, it asks what is used to <u>produce</u> energy. These resources include coal, gas, nuclear, wind, hydroelectric,

biomass, etc., as well as fuels that burn directly to produce energy such as wood or natural gas. The second approach to the question is to identify the <u>geographic source</u> of the energy materials. *Are the resources local, national, or from other countries? If the latter, exactly where do they come from?*

- Discuss the meaning of the unit title and how it might relate to the photo. The title assumes a global perspective in which many countries trade resources to supply their energy needs.

Exploring the Theme

15 mins

(pages 72–73)

- The opening spread features charts showing worldwide energy production and use in 1976 and thirty years later in 2006.

- Allow time for students to examine the charts, paying special attention to the keys and labels.

- Go over the charts together as a class to ensure that all students know how to interpret them. Ask: *What is shown on the left side of each chart?* (production) *On the right side?* (consumption) *Where are the figures for production by region found?* (on the outside curve on the left) *Where can you find production and use statistics for individual countries?* (on the central core) *What does the white area on the right of each chart show?* (energy consumed in international shipping)

- Have students work with a partner to find answers to the questions. In particular, have them compare production and consumption for each time period, and then compare the two graphs.

- Discuss question 2, comparing changes between 1976 and 2006. Students may want to compare the size of the colored areas or they could use numbers from the charts.

- Discuss question 3. Ask students to tell which regions produced more than they consumed in 2006 (Pacific, Russia/former U.S.S.R., Middle East, South America, and Africa) and which of these represents a change from 1976 (none—each of these regions produced more than they consumed in 1976 as well).

- In a class discussion, suggest that students look back to the infographic on page 10 that shows the enormous growth in affluence. Affluent people want more technology and labor-saving devices that in turn consume more energy.

TIP If students plan to take standardized international exams, they may encounter infographics like these as a prompt for an explanatory essay. This happens in the academic version of IELTS, for example. Ask how they would organize a comparison of the two charts.

Answer Key

Possible answers:

1. The charts show worldwide energy production and use in 1976 and 30 years later in 2006.
2. Reasons for change include industrialization and population growth—especially in developing countries—as well as growth in affluence and changes in technology. Asia shows the biggest change over 30 years.
3. The Middle East; despite increased consumption, the greatest difference between production and use is in the Middle East. In some oil-producing countries, populations are still relatively small.

IDEAS FOR . . . Expansion

Suggest that students keep an energy diary for two days. They make note of all the energy they consciously use and for how long. *How many lights do they burn* (are they using old incandescent bulbs that consume more energy and give off more heat than compact fluorescent or LED bulbs?), *what appliances do they use, how do they travel, how do they stay warm or cool,* etc. National Geographic has an initiative called *Great Energy Challenge* to help people learn more about their energy choices. Part of this program is an "Energy Diet" to reduce carbon consumption. This would be an effective follow-up to students' energy diaries. See **http://360energydiet.com/about-the-diet/**

Preparing to Read
(pages 74–75)

30 mins

WARM-UP

Some target vocabulary is presented in the context of a view of global warming and our need to consider alternatives to fossil fuels.

Ask: *What kinds of renewable energies are likely to provide viable alternatives to fossil fuels? What are the advantages and drawbacks to these sources of energy?*

Exercise A. | Building Vocabulary

- Have students find the words in blue in the reading and use the other words around them to guess their meanings.

- Remind students that looking at the part of speech can help them figure out the meaning. Clues from surrounding words identify the part of speech. For example, *prospect* is preceded by *the,* so it is clearly a noun. *Redefine* and *offset* have the infinitive form *to,* and *confirmed* is in the past tense, so all three are verbs.

- Allow time for students to complete the exercise individually.

Vocabulary Notes

Correspondingly means the same thing as *consistently* or *similarly*. It refers back to a previous statement and states that something is very similar or equivalent or in the same relationship as the previous reference.

When you *offset* something, you counteract the bad effect it has. You cancel out that bad effect by balancing it with something good. In environmental sciences, a *carbon offset* is a trade or credit towards something good to compensate for something bad, such as releasing more CO_2 emissions into the atmosphere. Governments, companies, and individuals all create CO_2 emissions or discharges that sometimes exceed the tolerable amount. When someone buys a *carbon offset,* they acknowledge that they have exceeded the allowable amounts of carbon pollution so they invest in something that will support the reduction of greenhouse gases in the atmosphere. Carbon offsets include supporting renewable energy (wind, solar, hydro), reforestation, or public awareness programs to promote green energy.

Word Partners

A *prospect* is a possibility that something may happen in the future. So the collocations *prospect of peace, prospect of war,* and *the prospect of having or being something* are likelihoods that something of the sort may happen. A person can also be regarded as a *prospect* if they are seen as someone who is expected to be important in the future.

Exercise B. | Building Vocabulary

- Students complete the sentences with words from the box. Encourage them to try matching words using the context before looking words up in a dictionary.
- Compare answers as a class.

Word Partners

If you do something *on behalf of* someone, you do it for the benefit of that person or in their interest. *The sports equipment sale was on behalf of the adaptive sports program that gives disabled people a chance to take part in sports.*

Exercise C. | Using Vocabulary

- Ask students to think about answers to the questions before talking with a partner about them.
- Ask pairs to share their responses with the class.

Word Link

The prefix *auto* means to do by one's self, so an *automobile* runs by itself, an *autobiography* is about the author's life, an *autograph* is a signature by the actual person, and *autonomy* for an individual means independence, while autonomy for a country means the freedom to govern itself.

Exercise D. | Predicting

- Students read the first and last paragraphs of the reading on pages 76–82 to discern the writer's purpose.
- Check the answer *after* students read the passage.

track **1-04** You may want to play the audio while students read. Remind students that the vocabulary definitions in the numbered footnotes at the bottom of the pages will help them understand the reading.

Overview of the Reading

Author Bill McKibben recapitulates how modern societies developed a dependence on fossil fuel energy, but he then asserts that we now face crucial decision points about continuing on this track. He cites both global warming and peak oil as situations we face now and argues that we cannot delay taking measures to reduce our CO_2 levels. The author states that in order to reduce carbon dioxide emissions to a viable level, we need a global halt to coal burning by 2030.

The original McKibben article and another by the same author appeared in a special energy issue of *National Geographic* in March 2009. For the source, see **http://ngm.nationalgeographic.com/2009/03/energy-challenge/mckibben-text**

Reading Infographics

As part of their preview of the reading, ask students to look at the photographs and read the captions. Ask: *Which photographs represent the current situation?* (Hong Kong harbor and the office building in Manhattan) *Which photos are innovative steps toward independence from fossil fuels?* (The wind turbines in Denmark and the solar panels in Nevada both harness renewable energy instead of fossil fuels.)

IDEAS FOR . . . Checking Comprehension

Ask: *What effects of global warming affect your life now? What about ten years from now if current trends continue?*

What do you think "peak oil" means? How likely is it that renewable resources (wind, water, biomass, etc.) can substitute for petroleum products where you live?

IDEAS FOR . . . Expansion

The Great Energy Challenge at National Geographic contains several interactive features where students can learn about the impact of their energy choices. At the human footprint website **http://education .nationalgeographic.com/education/media/human-footprint-interactive/?ar_a=1**, participants learn about the impact of things they ordinarily eat–eggs, bread, bananas–or use–cars, newspapers, showers–in terms of carbon footprints.

Understanding the Reading
(pages 83–85)

45 mins

Check students' predictions in exercise **D** on page 75.

Answer Key

b. to persuade

Before proceeding with the comprehension questions, ask the class if there were areas of the reading that they didn't understand. Write the letters of the paragraphs or problematic vocabulary on the board and return to them if they are not clarified in the comprehension activities.

Exercise A. | Identifying Main Ideas

- Ask students to read the questions and then quickly skim the identified paragraphs to match main ideas.
- Check the answers as a class, asking students to explain their choices.

Answer Key

1. H 2. D 3. A 4. J 5. G

Exercise B. | Identifying Key Details

- Ask students to underline no more than three key words in each question. Allow time for students to scan the reading for the information.
- Go over responses as a class, asking in which paragraph the detail was found.
- Note that most of the questions require students to give a reason or to explain a situation.

NOTE: Throughout this teacher's guide, letters in brackets are used to indicate the paragraph where the answer is found.

Answer Key

1. the industrial revolution [inferred from paragraph A] 2. 50 percent [E] 3. a sudden rise or sharp spike [F] 4. warmer air holds more water vapor [I] 5. the rapid melting of glaciers [I] 6. flooding [I] 7. 350 parts per million [J] 8. stop burning coal by 2030, use renewable fuels, not fossil fuels [K]

Exercise C. | Interpreting Charts

- Check that students understand the key word *emissions* in the title of the chart. An emission is something sent out into the air, in this case carbon dioxide from people's homes.
- Discuss other features of the chart, noting that regions of the world are color-coded and that each spoke represents a country, only some of which are identified. Measures of released CO_2 in kilograms are given next to the line for Kuwait. The large numbers indicate the position or rank on the chart.
- Ask students to think about the climates of countries in the top 10 group. Ask: *Which need heating and which use air conditioning during much of the year?*

Answer Key

1. Annual or yearly amounts of CO_2 released or leaked into the air from homes on a per person basis. **2.** Kuwait releases more CO_2 than other countries, but other countries in that region—Bahrain, the UAE—are not far behind. In these places, air conditioning is used for much of the year and houses are built so that cooled air leaks out. Moreover, fuel is cheap because it is produced locally, so there is little incentive for conservation. **3.** Some developing countries have lower emission rates than developed countries.

Exercise D. | Understanding a Process

- Students focus on a cause-effect chain described in paragraph H. Note that three letters have already been placed on the chart as markers. Students may dispute the placement of item "c" because there is reference to a second Arctic warming in the third sentence and no such reference at the end of the paragraph. In fact, it is that second warming that opened the ocean passages mentioned in item "d."

- After students complete the exercise, check answers as a class. Invite volunteers to read the sentence where they found answers to the items.

Answer Key

g→e→d→k→j→f→h→i→b→a→c;

Note: another acceptable order is:

g→e→c→d→k→j→f→h→i→b→a for reasons given above.

Exercise E. | Identifying Meaning from Context

- Encourage students to find the words or expressions and guess what they mean in the context of that paragraph. Only then should they return to the page and select the closest match.

- Students might want to create new sentences using these items for their vocabulary notebook.

Answer Key

1. d **2.** a **3.** b **4.** f **5.** c **6.** e

Vocabulary Notes

Ask about the *feedback loop* mentioned in paragraph H. In biology and environmental science, a feedback loop occurs when effects from one part of a process start to affect causes and therefore speed up the whole process. For example, when melting ice exposes more water, the water absorbs more heat from the sun and this in turn causes even more widespread melting.

CT Focus: Interpreting Figurative Language

- Go over the information in the **CT Focus** box. Literal language is when the meaning is the same as the meaning of the words themselves. By contrast, figurative language is when we use words to create an image using figures of speech or idioms.

- Start a discussion by mentioning familiar figures of speech and then asking the class for examples. You might use: *bed of roses, smooth as silk, cold feet, final straw, let the cat out of the bag, smiling moon,* or *dancing flowers.*

Exercise F. | Critical Thinking: Interpreting Figurative Language

Students select the best interpretation of figurative language from the reading. Ask the class to explain why one interpretation is better than the other.

Answer Key

1. a **2.** a **3.** b **4.** a **5.** b

Exercise G. | Critical Thinking: Evaluating Reasons

Students work with a partner to discuss the questions.

Answer Key

Answers will vary, but one reason is that figurative language adds color to writing by creating links with other areas of knowledge.

45 mins

Developing Reading Skills *(page 86)*

Reading Skill: Recognizing a Writer's Tone

- Explain that writers of scientific articles are expected to be objective and formal, logically supporting arguments with data and examples. However, writers in popular media such as magazines and blogs often write subjectively as they express a personal point of view and try to persuade readers to accept this perspective.

- Go over the information in the **Reading Skill** box, noting the clues to recognizing a writer's subjectivity.

Exercise A. | Identifying Tone

The exercise gives guided practice in identifying indications of subjectivity.

Answer Key

1. *of course* assuming agreement [A]
2. *two little problems* when the writer means two huge problems, sarcasm [D]
3. *little question where the future lies,* irony [F]
4. *all those old ferns and plankton,* sarcasm, and *Why wouldn't it cause problems?* irony [H]
5. *civilization-shaking,* use of strong, figurative language [I]
6. *we've* and *our,* use of personal pronouns [I]
7. *it's a crisis for this moment,* personal opinion [J]

IDEAS FOR . . . Expansion

Students who want to learn more about energy options can explore several sites:

http://www.nationalgeographic.com/earthpulse/ energy-and-carbon.html has a visual display of current and possible energy use.

Listen to a TED talk on 36 topics related to energy from behavioral changes that can modify personal energy consumption to renewable energy options. A list is at **http://www.ted.com/topics/energy** There is also a list of ten TED talks on the end of oil at **http:// www.ted.com/playlists/58/the_end_of_oil.html**

Get statistics and updates on energy production and consumption by countries of the world at **http://www .eia.gov/countries/**

Viewing: Powering Cities *(page 87)*

Overview of the Video

The designers of a new skyscraper in New York City wanted to create a building that would use half the energy of typical urban buildings. Their design filters air, uses rainwater as part of its water supply and to cool the building, and has special glass to let sunlight in but keep heat out. As a result, the innovative building at 1 Bryant Park has won awards for its environmental design.

Background Note

Buildings are among the greatest consumers of energy, particularly those located in temperate climates with cold winters and hot summers so that temperature modification is needed year round. Architects around the world are experimenting with building designs that cut the consumption of fossil fuels and take advantage of alternative energy. One of the most unusual is the Bahrain World Trade Center which captures wind energy with windmills attached to the towers. See **http://www.bahrainwtc.com/** for details. Several National Geographic sites have photographs of environmentally friendly green buildings. For example, see **http://news.nationalgeographic.com/news/2013/04/pictures/130419-extreme-green-building/**

Before Viewing

Exercise A. | Using a Dictionary

- Have students work individually to match the words and their definitions.
- Compare the answers as a class.

Answer Key

1. particulate **2.** circulate **3.** ventilation **4.** make a dent **5.** filter out

Vocabulary Notes

Literally, if you *make a dent* in something, you make a hollow or depression in the surface of something, like a car fender. But the saying is used as an idiom to mean that you make some progress on a big job or have a noticeable effect on a project. Used figuratively, it can also mean to reduce the amount of something. *The car repairs made a big dent in Karl's savings.*

Exercise B. | Thinking Ahead

Large buildings require heating or cooling, energy to run elevators, water supplies, and energy for telecommunications. Some possible ways to reduce consumption are to use solar panels, to collect rainwater, to have roof gardens to cool the building, and to block heat coming in through glass walls during the summer.

While Viewing

- Ask students to read the questions so they are prepared to watch and listen for certain information. They should underline the key information in each question.
- Play the video while students write short answers to the questions.

After Viewing

Exercise A.

- Have students work in pairs to discuss and compare answers.
- Ask students if there are any points that are unclear that they wish to discuss.

Answer Key

1. The building filters particulate matter from the air, so the released air is cleaner in the surrounding area.
2. It cuts water consumption and provides cooled water for the air conditioning system.
3. A special frit pattern built into the glass allows sunlight in but keeps heat out.

Exercise B. | Critical Thinking: Synthesizing

So far, "green buildings" are the exception, and most urban construction has not changed. Buildings such as the one in the video serve as examples of what can be done, but until they become economically advantageous, very little will change. If large cities experience cutbacks in electricity, perhaps this will be an incentive to create buildings that are more sustainable.

Exploring Written English *(page 88–90)*

45 mins

- Read aloud the writing goal. Writing summary essays requires students to separate the main topics from the details.

- Remind students that writing is a process. Just as there are stages of reading or viewing that lead to comprehension, there are stages in the writing process that lead to producing a final draft. The lesson reviews language for writing, and then presents the steps in the writing process.

- Remind students about the Independent Student Handbook at the back of their Student Book. Pages 246–248 have useful tips on academic writing and research. Paraphrasing, the **Language for Writing** topic for this unit, is discussed on page 249.

Exercise A.

- Go over the information and examples in the **Language for Writing** box.

- *Plagiarism* is using someone else's work and passing it off as your own. It is an ethical problem in academics and journalism where it is considered seriously dishonest. This section focuses on using synonyms to avoid plagiarism. Another strategy is to quote directly and give sources for any information used.

- Check to make sure that students are familiar with a thesaurus and how it works. A *thesaurus* is a reference guide that gives a range of synonyms for a word. Remind students that although synonyms have the same general meaning, there are shades of differences in how they are used. Therefore, while a thesaurus is very helpful in providing possible substitutions for a word, it will be up to the individual to determine whether the suggested words are appropriate.

- Some students may be familiar with *Roget's Thesaurus* in its print or online version. In word processors, right click on a word to find synonyms and thesaurus entries.

- Exercises **A** and **B** provide practice in choosing appropriate synonyms for the context.

Answer Key

1. b. far-off
2. c. repeated
3. c. contemplated

IDEAS FOR . . . Further Research

Suggest that students look up the target vocabulary from page 74 in a thesaurus to find synonyms. Looking at how the words were used in the context of page 74, which synonyms would be suitable? Things to consider include shades of meaning, collocations with other words, and the formal or informal context of the passage.

Exercise B. | Applying

Students replace words in the sentences with synonyms and alter the sentence structure to accommodate other parts of speech.

Answer Key

Answers will vary.

Writing Skill: Writing a Summary

- Have students read the information in the box.

- A summary will be a condensed version of the original passage with emphasis on the main ideas and intent of the writing. Emphasize that students should be able to identify and restate the main points in their own words.

Exercise C. | Critical Thinking: Evaluating

Students read two summaries and use criteria to decide which is better.

Answer Key

Example "b" is superior because it is shorter but conveys the same ideas as the original using different words.

Exercise D. | Brainstorming

- Unlike earlier exercises with brainstorming, this one is meant to activate memories of the main points of the reading passage.

- Students work with a partner to identify the main points for each of the five areas of the chart.

Exercise E. | Taking Notes

Students reread the article on pages 76–82 to check their memories of the main points. They take notes about points they missed or forgot and use the notes to make corrections in the chart.

Exercise F. | Vocabulary for Writing

Following the discussion of a writer's tone on page 86, students sort words according to whether they are objective or subjective.

Writing Task: Drafting
(page 91)

Exercise A. | Planning

- Point out that this planning chart is a useful way to organize ideas before writing.
- Go over the four steps in the exercise, noting that there will be an introduction, three body paragraphs, and a conclusion.
- Point out that complete sentences are not necessary for the details and notes in the planning chart. The important thing is to get some ideas down on paper.
- Allow time for students to complete their charts.

Exercise B. | Draft 1

Remind students that the purpose of a first draft is to get ideas down on paper. They will have time to revise and edit later.

Writing Task: Revising
(pages 92–93)

Exercise C. | Critical Thinking: Analyzing

- Explain that analyzing this model essay will help students to revise their own writing.
- Point out how the organization of this essay follows the original article but emphasizes just the main points.

Exercise D. | Revising

Explain that these steps will help students to reread their work carefully and look for ways to improve it.

Exercise E. | Peer Evaluation

- Remind students that this process will help students to see if they have organized their ideas clearly.
- Ensure that both members of the pair have equal time to give feedback.

Writing Task: Editing
(page 94)

Exercise F. | Draft 2

Walk around and monitor students as they work. Provide assistance as needed.

Exercise G. | Editing Practice

- Go over the information in the box.
- Allow time for students to find and correct the mistakes.
- Invite volunteers to write the corrected sentences on the board.

Answer Key

1. *use* instead of *feeding*

2. *be exhausted, used up,* or *depleted* instead of *escape*

3. *reduction* instead of *refusal*

Exercise H. | Editing Checklist

- Read aloud the sentences in the editing checklist.
- Allow time for students to read and edit their work.

Exercise I. | Final Draft

- Allow time for students to work on their final draft (or set this for homework).

- Collect students' work.
- Let them know when they can expect to get their essays back. At that time, be sure to go over the marking system that you use.

IDEAS FOR . . . Further Research

Suggest that students project what effect changes in energy will have on their lives in twenty years. What things that they do or use now will be more or less the same? What things will be radically different? Have them write down their ideas and put them somewhere where they can find them years from now and check their predictions.

Working Together

Academic Track
Life Science/Sociology

Academic Pathways:
Lesson A: Identifying subjects
in complex sentences
Evaluating sources
Lesson B: Organizing a comparative essay
Writing a comparative essay

Unit Theme

Unit 5 explores swarm intelligence, the idea that when animals, people, and robots work together cooperatively in self-organizing systems, there are advantages for both individuals and the group.

Think and Discuss *(page 95)*

5 mins

- Ask students to describe the photo. Ask: *What do you see in the photo? What activity is going on here? How does a stock market work?*

- The photograph shows the floor of a stock exchange with individual traders looking at boards that display the latest prices for stocks. Individual traders make decisions to buy, sell, or hold onto stocks based on trends in the price of individual stocks as well as how the whole stock market is moving at that moment. Traders have to act quickly to take advantage of good prices. Sometimes the value of the stocks will rise overall, a bull market. Conversely, a bear market is when the entire market falls. If this happens too much or too suddenly, it is described as a stock market crash, something that has only happened a few times, fortunately.

- Discuss possible answers to questions 1 and 2. The questions are subjective, so individual responses may differ. Start with an example of heavy traffic during a rain storm. Individual drivers slow down as they see the mass of other drivers decreasing their speed due to the weather and driving conditions. If an accident causes a *bottleneck*—a narrow area that all drivers must go through—the crowd of drivers works together so that the whole stream eventually gets through.

- Other examples might include the way crowds behave at a sporting event or a rock concert. Ask: *How does a particular movement get started so that everyone joins in? What is group thinking? Do most people prefer to do what everyone else is doing or act independently?*

- Discuss the meaning of the unit title and how it might relate to the photo.

Exploring the Theme

15 mins

(pages 96–97)

- The opening spread shows construction workers in Tunisia transporting supplies to the top of a building using a human chain.

- Allow time for students to study the photograph and read the text on the left before asking them to work with a partner to answer the questions.

- For question 1, each person in the chain moves within a limited range to take the item from the person below and give it to the person above. The material moves upward, but the people do not have to carry material up the side of the building. It is an effective low-technology solution. By contrast, in mechanized building sites, a crane or other machine is used to transport one item at a time to the top of the building.

- In discussing question 2, ask: *How did primitive people hunt large animals?* Archaeology shows that groups often worked cooperatively to drive large animals such as bison or mammoths over a cliff. The people formed long lines to "funnel" the animals in a particular direction towards the edge of a cliff.

- For question 3, ask: *How do articles appear in Wikipedia? Can social media be used to solve problems? How does crowdfunding work?*

Answer Key

Possible answers:

1. Each participant does his part so that the group gets work accomplished with less energy used.
2. Primitive people often worked together to hunt or take advantage of other food sources. Some members of the social group took care of children or elderly people who could not participate.
3. Answers will vary but may include examples of crowdsourcing to solve problems or crowdfunding to raise money for a common cause.

IDEAS FOR . . .   Expansion

Ask students to think of an example of crowdsourcing that uses social media. For example, can they think of a search for a lost person or pet where people from many different places who didn't know each other contributed information?

Genealogy is an area where many people share information on family history with people they have never met. Use keywords *crowdsourcing* and *genealogy* together to find sites and examples.

Do students know of creative projects that emerged from crowdsourcing? For example, the National Geographic documentary film *Life in a Day* was created with 80,000 submissions to the YouTube video-sharing site with 4500 hours of film footage from people in 192 countries. Learn more at: **http://movies .nationalgeographic.com/movies/life-in-a-day/**

You can watch the trailer and the film at **https://www .youtube.com/user/lifeinaday**

Preparing to Read

30 mins *(pages 98–99)*

WARM-UP

Some target vocabulary is presented in a reading about new technologies based on how insects move. These tiny devices could be used in dangerous environments such as warfare instead of people taking risks.

Ask students if they have ever tried to catch an insect that seemed to sense their presence and quickly move away.

Exercise A. | Building Vocabulary

- Have students find the words in blue in the reading and use the other words around them to guess their meanings.
- Remind students that looking at the part of speech can help them figure out the meaning. Clues from surrounding words identify the part of speech. For example, *capabilities, simulation,* and *defense* are all nouns because of their use in the sentences. *Emergent* and *unpredictable* are adjectives that modify other words, and *precisely*—ending in *ly*—is an adverb modifying the insects' motion.

Vocabulary Notes

Emerge means to come forth or to rise out of a hidden place so that something is visible. The related word *emergent* refers to something that is coming into being or coming into view. Thus an *emergent technology* is a new way of doing things or an innovation that is just starting to be used.

Answer Key

1. defense
2. manipulate
3. simulation
4. capabilities
5. unpredictable
6. emergent
7. precisely

Exercise B. | Building Vocabulary

- Students complete the sentences with words from the box. Encourage them to try to match words with the context before looking words up in a dictionary.
- Compare answers as a class.

Vocabulary Notes

Two of the words in the box are part of pairs of opposites. If something like government is *centralized*, it is concentrated in a single place. By contrast, a *decentralized* government is distributed over a wide area with local centers. If information is *relevant*, it is closely connected to the situation. However, if the data are *irrelevant*, they are not related or important for this topic.

Answer Key

1. declare 2. relevant 3. coordinate 4. decentralized
5. Complementary

Word Usage

The box describes two words that sound the same and are alike except for one crucial letter. *Complementary* with an "e" refers to two or more things that go well together. A way to remember the spelling is that one thing helps to comp**le**te the other. When you give a *compliment* with an "i," you say something *n**i**ce* to praise someone. *Complimentary* with an "i" has this sense of admiration. *Complimentary* also can mean free, as collocated with *complimentary tickets*.

Exercise C. | Using Vocabulary

- Ask students to think about answers to the questions before talking with a partner about them.
- Ask pairs to share their responses with the class.

Answer Key

Answers will vary, but students may respond to the first question by saying that in a group, strengths offset weaknesses.

2. In a choral group, singers have different talents or skills that complement each other. These might be vocal quality, range, sense of intonation, or ability to sight read.
3. New types of smartphones emerge all the time that have capabilities that replace older technologies such as digital cameras or video cameras.

IDEAS FOR . . . Expansion

Ask students to think about a time when they bought a type of emergent technology that was so new on the market that few people had one. Ask: *How did you learn about it? Why did you decide to take a chance on something innovative instead of waiting until it became better known? What was your experience with this product?*

Exercise D. | Brainstorming

- Students work in groups of three or four to discuss the questions.
- Bring the class together and ask for specific examples.

Answer Key

Answers will vary.

Exercise E. | Predicting

- Have students look at the photographs (and read the captions) on pages 100–105 and read the first and last paragraphs.
- Students predict what animal behavior and human activities the passage will cover.
- Check the answers *after* students read the passage.

 track **1-05** You may want to play the audio while students read. Remind students that the vocabulary definitions in the numbered footnotes at the bottom of pages will help them understand the reading.

Overview of the Reading

Peter Miller, the author of the reading, is a senior editor at *National Geographic.* During his 25 year career there, he has been involved with a wide variety of topics in many disciplines, so he is familiar with both animal and human behaviors.

Miller writes about swarm intelligence, groups of many individuals who coordinate their actions according to three principles. First, control is decentralized and each individual acts separately. Second, the organism reacts in response to things right around it, such as movement of a neighboring organism. Third, the rules are very simple: Move with the crowd. Using these three principles, a group—whether ants, fish, caribou, or people—can quickly respond to change and danger.

The original article appeared in July 2007 and can be found at **http://ngm.nationalgeographic.com/2007/07/swarms/miller-text** Field notes by Miller can be found at the same site.

Key Concepts

Swarming behavior is a feature of ant and bee colonies. Some of the early research on ant social behavior was conducted by E. O. Wilson, the Harvard sociobiologist. Over the years, *National Geographic* has published many articles and videos on both ants and bees. To learn more about these social insects, go to the main sites at **http://animals.nationalgeographic.com/animals/bugs/ant/** and **http://animals.nationalgeographic.com/animals/bugs/honeybee/**

IDEAS FOR . . . Checking Comprehension

Ask students the following question about the reading, or write it on the board.

You looked at the unit photographs when you previewed the reading passage. How do the photos of butterflies, fish, reindeer, and robots fit the idea of swarm intelligence? Explain your answer.

IDEAS FOR . . . Expansion

A short article by Elizabeth Snodgrass suggests that swarm intelligence may soon be used to regulate the movement of traffic, either with cars on the ground or with airplanes in the skies. Use the article to elicit a response from students about whether they think this will happen soon or not. Ask them to give reasons to support their point of view. The link is **http://ngm.nationalgeographic.com/2007/07/swarms/did-you-know-learn**

 # Understanding the Reading

45 mins *(pages 106–108)*

Check students' predictions in exercise **E** on page 99.

Answer Key

1. butterflies, fish, bees, reindeer
2. migration, attacks by predators, survival in the cold
3. Google, Wikipedia, robots, swarming behavior, crowdsourcing
4. The purpose of the article is to show how studying smart swarming behavior could help humans.

Before proceeding with the comprehension questions, ask the class if there were areas of the reading that they didn't understand. Write the letters of the paragraphs or problematic vocabulary on the board and return to them if they are not clarified in the comprehension activities.

Exercise A. | Identifying Main Ideas

- Ask students to read the questions. If necessary, have them look back at the passage and reread the relevant paragraphs.

- Check the answers as a class and ask students to explain their choices by referring to lettered paragraphs in the text.

NOTE: Throughout this teacher's guide, letters in brackets are used to indicate the paragraph where the answer is found.

Answer Key

1. It is a group of individuals who act together to give the group the ability to cope with change or danger. [B]
2. Individuals in a group are more likely to avoid predators, locate food and mates, and move long distances successfully. [O–Q, X–Z]
3. distributed leadership, act on local information, and have simple rules [C, G, R]
4. Google uses the collective intelligence of all Internet users to rank sources by the number of hits; knowledgeable experts collaborate by contributing and correcting Wikipedia articles. [U, V]

Exercise B. | Identifying Purpose

- Allow time for students to write their answers individually.
- After students complete the exercise, check answers as a class.

Answer Key

1. [T–V] 2. [R] 3. [W] 4. [O–Q] 5. [B–C] 6. [D–N]

Exercise C. | Identifying Meaning from Context

- Encourage students to find the words or expressions and guess what they mean in the context of the lettered paragraph. Only then should they return to the page and complete the sentences.
- Students might want to create new sentences using these items for their vocabulary notebook.

Answer Key

1. d 2. c 3. f 4. g 5. a 6. e 7. b

Exercise D. | Summarizing Key Details

- Students reread paragraphs B to N to find concepts to complete the concept map.
- Remind students that they used a concept map in Unit 3. This type of graphic organizer is helpful in organizing information from a text.

Answer Key

Example in the Animal World: pigeons, leader, pigeons nearby [B and C] **Entertainment:** (2) fly in direction of nearby birds, (3) stay close to nearby birds [D]
Robot Teams: Advantages: take its place [F]; Rules: use local information [G]; Examples: foot bots; hand bots; eye bots; information [I]; Military uses: prisoners [M]; fires or earthquakes [H and M]; hazardous waste [M]

CT Focus: Evaluating Sources

Go over the information in the **CT Focus** box. As noted earlier, the writer of the reading passage is not himself an expert in the field of swarm intelligence, but an editor who is familiar with many of the issues in the article. To research the article, he consulted with many experts whose credentials he cites to support his ideas.

Exercise E. | Critical Thinking: Evaluating Sources

- Individual students scan the reading passage to locate the quotes.
- Then, working with a partner, students discuss what the quotes mean, making a connection between the quote and the person's expertise.
- Compare responses as a class, asking students to support their ideas with examples.

Answer Key

Note: Credentials are listed with the paragraph where the quote is found.
Quote 1: [G] Vijay Kumar, professor of mechanical engineering at the University of Pennsylvania; He talks about the three principles of swarm intelligence in biology; **Quote 2:** [P] Daniel Grünbaum, a biologist at the University of Washington; He's a biologist talking about fish and predators; **Quote 3:** [V] Thomas Malone, at the MIT Center for Collective Intelligence; Wikipedia is an example of the types of swarm intelligence his center studies.
Question 2: a. Grünbaum; b. Malone; c. Kumar

Exercise F. | Critical Thinking: Analyzing Information

Working in a small group, students discuss the role of the individual as presented in paragraph W.

Answer Key

Answers will vary, but basically each individual has a responsibility to act responsibly and make their own decisions.

> TIP   Sociologists and social psychologists have a
> more negative view of crowds when they
> talk about *crowd* or *mob psychology*. It is characteristic
> that individuals within a mob give up responsibility for
> their actions and are swayed by the emotional intensity
> of the group. While some crowds can show positive
> emotional intensity, such as religious experiences or a
> civil rights demonstration, other groups are aggressive,
> become violent, and often riot.

Developing Reading Skills

(page 109)

45 mins

Reading Skill: Identifying Subjects in Complex Sentences

The skill entails distinguishing the main clauses of a sentence from the dependent clauses, participial phrases, and prepositional phrases. Suggest that students use different colored markers to indicate these sentence components.

Exercise A. | Identifying Subjects in Complex Sentences

Students first identify the main clauses and then circle a one-word subject.

Answer Key

Note: The main clause is given and the subject is underlined.

1. Marco Dorigo's group in Brussels is leading a European effort
2. The result was a convincing simulation
3. [A] smart swarm is a group of individuals
4. generic birdlike objects were each given three instructions
5. News spreads quickly
6. the ingredients of smart group behavior add up

Exercise B. | Applying

Students repeat the process for paragraphs K, M, T, U, and W.

Answer Key

Note: The main clause is given and the subject is underlined.

[K] 1. the foot-long (30 cm) red robots pivoted 2. each robot searched for objects 3. it used wireless network gear
[M] 1. The demonstration was part of the Centibots project 2. teams of robots might someday be sent 3. Military agencies have funded a number of robotics programs
[T] 1. groups have already adopted tactics 2. activists used mobile communications devices
[U] 1. Google surveys billions of Web pages 2. It ranks them 3. The pages are listed first 4. Google says
[W] 1. thoughts underline truth 2. A group won't be smart 3. it relies on its members 4. the bottom line is that our actions matter

---

IDEAS FOR . . .   Expansion

Students who want to explore some of the applications of swarm intelligence mentioned in the reading can use the links at **http://ngm .nationalgeographic.com/2007/07/swarms/swarm-theory-learn** These sites include the boids, Centibots, and the MIT Center for Collective Intelligence.

Another source is a TED talk by Jens Krause, who shows simulations with robotfish and human subjects responding to collective intelligence. View it at

http://tedxtalks.ted.com/video/Swarm-Intelligence-Jens-Krause

Viewing: Locust Swarm *(page 110)*

Overview of the Video

In 1875, huge clouds of locusts destroyed crops in the Central Plains of the United States. The insects appeared suddenly, did their damage, and then disappeared. For over a century, their disappearance has been a mystery. Using ice cores from the Rocky Mountains, researcher Jeff Lockwood found locusts from the 19th century and formed a hypothesis about their disappearance. He attributes the vanished locusts to farmers tilling the soil—and thus disrupting locust nests of eggs—at the time of the Gold Rush.

Background Note

Swarms or plagues of locusts are mentioned from the earliest recorded history throughout the world. The voracious insects appear in huge numbers and eat all the vegetation in their path. As a result, farmers have no crops to eat or food for their animals, so the farmers and animals either die or have to move away. People left diary accounts and letters from the great swarm of 1875 in the United States and some of these can be read on **http://www.hearthstonelegacy.com/when-the-skies-turned-to-black-the_locust-plague-of-1875.htm**

Today, swarms of locusts are still a problem in many places, especially in Africa and Pakistan. The Food and Agriculture Organization of United Nations maintains a locust watch. Updates are available on **http://www.fao.org/ag/locusts/en/info/info/index.html** Researchers at Oxford University are trying to understand how a locust swarm starts. A video on their research is at **http://video.nationalgeographic.com/video/animals/bugs-animals/grasshoppers/locust_research/**

Before Viewing

Exercise A. | Using a Dictionary

- Have students work individually to match the words and their definitions.
- Compare the answers as a class.
- Ask students to predict how these words will be used in the video.

Vocabulary Notes

Plague used as a noun refers to a fatal infectious disease, the bubonic plague, which killed many people throughout history. The Black Death in the 14th century was a *pandemic*—an epidemic on a global scale—that killed about a third of the world's population. *Plague* as a verb means to cause continual trouble or distress as the swarms of locusts do.

Exercise B. | Thinking Ahead

Locusts are a type of grasshopper, but other insects that devour crops are beetles and caterpillars. In addition, some insects such as mosquitoes spread diseases including malaria, yellow fever, and dengue.

While Viewing

- Suggest that students read the questions so they are prepared to watch and listen for certain information. They should underline the key information in each question.
- As students watch, they take very brief notes, just enough to answer the questions or remind them what the answer was after viewing.
- Allow enough time for students to complete their answers. Ask if anyone needs to watch the video again.

After Viewing

Exercise A.

- Have students work in pairs to discuss and compare answers.
- Ask students if there are any points that are unclear that they wish to discuss.

Exercise B. | Critical Thinking: Synthesizing

Like many other social insects, locusts live in decentralized groups, pay attention to the movements of surrounding locusts, and have very simple rules. Using this swarm intelligence helped them cover a lot of ground and eat a lot of food. It might be useful to play the video again so students can focus on the movements of the locust swarms.

Exploring Written English
(pages 111–114)

45 mins

- Read aloud the writing goal. Comparing two or more things is a common writing task. Sometimes the form is called comparison-contrast. When you compare, you focus on similarities whereas contrasting emphasizes the differences.

- Remind students that writing is a process. Just as there are stages of reading or viewing that lead to comprehension, there are stages in the writing process that lead to producing a final draft. The lesson starts with brainstorming, then goes on to review of language for writing, and then presents the steps in the writing process.

- Remind students about the Independent Student Handbook at the back of their Student Book. Pages 246–248 have useful tips on academic writing and research. On page 248, there is a list of terms used to outline contrasting views.

Exercise A. | Brainstorming

Brainstorming is a useful first step for getting ideas before writing. In this case, students work in pairs to think of how members of groups collaborate or work together to achieve something.

Exercise B. | Planning

If students need further information on how specific animals collaborate, suggest that they visit **http://animals.nationalgeographic.com/animals/** and use the pull-down list on the right to locate the animal they seek.

Exercise C. | Vocabulary for Writing

- Have students locate the words in the lettered paragraphs of the main reading and guess their meanings from context before using the words to complete the sentences.

- Check answers as a class, asking students to use each word in a new sentence.

Answer Key

1. synchronized **2.** Collective intelligence **3.** cope with **4.** dependent on **5.** self-organizing **6.** interacting

Free Writing

- Remind students that free writing is writing rapidly to come up with ideas without worrying about mistakes.

- Set a time limit of five minutes for students to free write about an example of human cooperative behavior. Encourage students to use vocabulary from exercise **C.**

Exercise D.

- Go over the information and examples in the **Language for Writing** box.

- Parallel structure gives writing a polish and clarifies meaning.

- It is advisable to use parallel structure when you have two or more adjectives, noun phrases, or verb phrases in a sentence. Sometimes you will have to change the part of speech in order to create parallelisms.

- The exercise gives practice in creating parallel structure.

Answer Key

1. quick **2.** communicate **3.** animals herding, birds flocking **4.** helping **5.** how they avoid predators

Exercise E.

Students return to their free writing and add at least one parallel structure.

Writing Skill: Organizing a Comparative Essay

- Have students read the information in the box, noting that they have two equally valid ways to organize their essay.

- Emphasize that the thesis statement is the unifying element in an essay. It states the main ideas and the order in which they will be developed in body paragraphs, but each of these paragraphs must include additional details and examples to develop the key concepts.

Exercise F. | Critical Thinking: Analyzing

Students analyze some preliminary notes for a comparison essay.

Vocabulary Notes

The biological order of *primates* includes humans, the great apes (chimpanzees, gorillas, orangutans, and gibbons), New and Old World monkeys, tarsiers, lemurs, and lorises. Therefore, the category "nonhuman primate" contains a great diversity of animals that are more different than alike in any of the points of comparison in these notes.

Answer Key

1. humans and nonhuman primates
2. living groups, learning, use of tools
3. The block outline would discuss features of humans in the first body paragraph, and then features of nonhuman primates in the second body paragraph. Using the point-by-point method, the first body paragraph would compare living arrangements between the two groups, the second body paragraph would discuss learning, and the third body paragraph would deal with tool making and use.
4. Further examples are needed for group composition, learning, communication, and toolmaking. Food sharing could be a separate topic, perhaps associated with diet and hunting.

Writing Task: Drafting
(page 115)

IDEAS FOR . . .   Preliminary Organization

Several graphic organizers are useful in organizing data for a comparison essay. If two or three subjects are being compared, suggest using a Venn diagram where overlapping areas indicate points of similarity, and where information in each circle is unique to the individual subject. A concept map or word web may be helpful in developing details for each of the discussion topics. Lastly, the T-chart on page 111 is another way to visually display ideas and their relationships before starting to write.

Exercise A. | Planning

- Students decide which organization method to use.
- Go over the seven steps in the exercise, noting that there will be a different number of body paragraphs, depending on the method of organization.
- Complete sentences are not necessary for the details and notes in the planning chart. The important thing is to get some ideas down on paper.
- Allow time for students to complete their charts, using ideas from exercise **A (Brainstorming)** and **Free Writing** as appropriate.
- Move around the class while students are writing, offering help and advice as needed. In particular, look for places where more details or examples would be desirable.
- Ask one or two students to read their thesis statement aloud to the class.

Exercise B. | Draft 1

Remind students that the purpose of a first draft is to get ideas down on paper. They will have time to revise and edit later.

Writing Task: Revising
(pages 116–117)

Exercise C. | Critical Thinking: Analyzing

- Explain that analyzing this model essay will help students to revise their own writing.
- Suggest that students read the essay individually before they analyze it with a partner.
- In the introduction, the author makes it clear that both honeybees and ants utilize collective intelligence. The thesis statement identifies the three areas of comparison.
- Ask the class how the writer makes use of authorities and how they are cited in the paper. The individual scholars mentioned and the publication dates give support of recent research to the article.

Answer Key

1. The thesis statement is the last sentence in the first paragraph and its key words are *roles, communication systems, learning.*
2. The order of ideas in the thesis statement is followed in the body paragraphs as the writer is using point-by-point organization. The first sentence in each paragraph is the topic sentence.
3. The key words from the thesis statement—*specific roles, sophisticated communication systems,* and *capable of learning*—are repeated in the topic sentences with the words slightly modified.
4. Some examples include the following: **body paragraph 1:** roles (and numbers) of queens, fertile males, sterile females, and the function of each group; **body paragraph 2:** pheromones and dances with explanation of how each is used for communication; **body paragraph 3:** examples of bees learning and ants both learning and teaching other ants

Exercise D. | Revising

Explain that these steps will help students to reread their work carefully and look for ways to improve it.

Exercise E. | Peer Evaluation

- Remind students that this process will help students to see if they have organized their ideas clearly.
- Ensure that both members of the pair have equal time to give feedback.

Writing Task: Editing
(page 118)

Exercise F. | Draft 2

Walk around and monitor students as they work. Provide assistance as needed.

Exercise G. | Editing Practice

The information in the box focuses on parallel structure and the importance of using the same part of speech, even if it entails paraphrasing.

Answer Key

1. The robots were programmed to look for anything pink and to avoid running into each other.
2. Coyotes and wolves are similar in terms of how they choose a leader and hunt together.
3. The robots are quick, responsive, and impossible to detect.
4. Ants survive by cooperating and making group decisions.

Exercise H. | Editing Checklist

- Read aloud the sentences in the editing checklist.
- Allow time for students to read and edit their work.

Exercise I. | Final Draft

- Allow time for students to work on their final draft (or set this for homework).
- Collect students' work.
- Let them know when they can expect to get their essays back. At that time, be sure to go over the marking system that you use.

IDEAS FOR . . . Further Research

This unit discusses many applications of swarm intelligence to everyday life, scientific experiments, and military situations, but it does not mention the legacy of the concept in science fiction writing as far back as the 1930s. See **http://en.wikipedia.org/wiki/Swarm_intelligence** for guides to the literature. Looking ahead, note that science fiction is the topic of Unit 10 in the Student Book.

Language and Culture

Academic Track
Interdisciplinary

Academic Pathways:
Lesson A: Inferring an author's attitude
           Understanding verbal phrases
Lesson B: Writing introductions and conclusions
           Writing a personal opinion essay

Unit Theme

Unit 6 explores the relationship between language and culture. It suggests that you experience a society differently when you know the language.

Think and Discuss *(page 119)*

5 mins

- Ask students to describe the photo. Ask: *What do you see in the photo? What activity is going on here? How do you think teaching and learning happen in this classroom?*

- The photograph shows Chinese schoolgirls reading books in class. The students wear uniforms and sit at separate desks, giving the impression that the classroom is organized in a traditional way. One girl looks directly into the camera while the other two seem focused on their reading.

- Discuss possible answers to questions 1 and 2. The questions are subjective, so individual responses may differ. Start by asking about the students' first language and languages they have learned, because these factors may contribute to their responses.

- Today, using the Internet is one of the main reasons for learning another language, especially English. Other reasons include travel, employment, and being able to communicate globally with people in your particular field.

- Difficulties depend on the languages. For example, sometimes language learning involves a new writing system, orthography, or learning a tonal language. Other potential problems are learning to recognize and produce different sounds, or adjusting to many different varieties of a language.

- Discuss the meaning of the unit title and how it might relate to the photo. Ask students to talk about their personal experiences in language learning.

Exploring the Theme
(pages 120–121)

15 mins

- The opening spread shows young children in Mongolia sitting with their dolls and stuffed animals in front of a painted mural of people wearing traditional costumes.

- For decades, linguists and psychologists have debated the *critical period hypothesis,* the idea that language—or at least some elements of language such as grammar or a near-native accent—are best learned at an early age. Much of the research has focused on learning a first language, and specialists in second language acquisition are not sure that the process is the same for learning an additional language after the first one. Some linguists, such as Steven Pinker, believe that physical changes in the brain make language learning more difficult after puberty, roughly the start of the teenage years. As a result, many parents are eager to have their children start learning another language at an early age.

- Allow time for students to study the photograph and read the text on the right before asking them to work with a partner to answer the questions.

- In discussing questions 2 and 3, ask: *Are there advantages to learning another language when you are an adult? Explain. What methodologies for language learning are used with young learners as contrasted with adults? What methods work best for you as a young adult?*

- In some countries, all second language learning with preschool children is done orally, using songs, games, videos, and play-like activities. This approach is based on ideas about childhood developmental stages as well as a desire not to interfere with the development of literacy in the child's first language.

Answer Key

Possible answers:

Essentially, the answers for all three questions are based on the critical period idea, that until puberty when changes occur in the brain, children are innately able to learn languages with greater fluency and accuracy than they can later in life. For question 3, point out the importance of motivation, something most young learners lack. Learning a language because you have a reason to use it can be highly motivating.

IDEAS FOR . . . Expansion

Ask students about the language learning policies in their countries. Ask: *Are students monolingual, or do they start to learn another language from an early age? Is this due to parental choice or government policy? When is English introduced in the curriculum now? Is this different from when you were in primary school?*

Preparing to Read
(pages 122–123)

30 mins

WARM-UP

Target vocabulary is contained within a description of attitudes towards reading fiction. Recent research suggests that reading fiction may have a beneficial effect on the brain.

Ask students about books they like to read for pleasure. Ask: *What types of books do you like to read?* (Some fiction categories include mysteries, romances, science fiction, and adventure novels.) *What is it about these kinds of books that you find appealing?*

Exercise A. | Building Vocabulary

- Have students find the words in blue in the reading and use other words around them to guess their meanings.

- Remind students that looking at the part of speech can help them figure out the meaning. Clues from surrounding words identify the part of speech. In this case, most of the target words are adjectives used to modify nouns. The exception is the phrase *on the contrary,* used to introduce a contrasting idea. Other words or phrases that signal contrasting ideas include *however, by contrast,* and *on the other hand.*

- Allow time for students to complete the exercise individually.

- Note that *straightforward* and *unintelligible* are extreme opposites.

Answer Key

1. on the contrary
2. monotonous
3. straightforward
4. definitive
5. nostalgic
6. irresistible
7. unintelligible

Word Link

The prefix *in-* has the effect of negating the base word. However, before letters *r, l,* and *m,* the *n* changes to match the word's starting letter, resulting in a double consonant. Examples are *irresistible, illiterate,* and *immaterial.* The *im-* form is also used to negate base words starting with *p* such as *imperfect, impractical,* and *imprecise.*

IDEAS FOR . . . Expansion

Suggest that students work in groups of four to think of words starting with *r, l, m,* and *p* that can be negated in this way. Each group can "test" another group to see if they can form the negatives and describe what the words mean. Hint: It may be helpful to use a dictionary for ideas.

Exercise B. | Building Vocabulary

- Students complete the sentences with words from the box. Encourage them to try to match words with the context before looking words up in a dictionary.
- Compare answers as a class.

Word Link

The prefix *con-* comes from a Latin word that means together, so words that start with *con-* have that as part of their meaning. If you make a *concerted* effort to get something done, two or more people work together on the project. If you have a business trip and vacation *concurrently,* you do both things together at the same time. If birds *congregate* on a beach, they come together.

Word Link

Something *cryptic* has a hidden meaning, so if you *encrypt* a message, you write it in a code that is secret. In computer science if you *encrypt* a file, only authorized people can access it and use it.

Exercise C. | Using Vocabulary

- Ask students to think about answers to the questions before talking with a partner about them.
- Ask pairs to share their responses with the class.

Exercise D. | Brainstorming

- Students work in groups of three or four to discuss the question.

- Have students explain why this way of learning has worked for them. Suggest that each person try one new way to build vocabulary for a week.

Exercise E. | Predicting

- Have students read the first and last paragraphs of the passage on pages 124–127 to guess what sort of reading this is.
- Check their answers *after* students read the passage.

track **1-06** You may want to play the audio while students read. Remind students that the vocabulary definitions in the numbered footnotes at the bottom of the pages will help them understand the reading.

Overview of the Reading

Daisy Zamora recalls her early experiences in learning English, first from her grandmother and later at school. Living in a Spanish-speaking country, she learned English from literature and listening to English songs. When she visited teenage cousins in the United States, Zamora learned that her English was not the same as theirs. This discovery provided the incentive to learn a vernacular form of English so that she could participate in their culture.

Background

Daisy Zamora is a contemporary poet from Nicaragua. She was raised in a cosmopolitan family that was active in politics. After university, she too became an activist against the dictator who ruled her country in the 1970s. Although at times Zamora was exiled to other countries in Central America, she later became active in the Ministry of Culture for the new government.

Zamora writes in Spanish, but her work has been translated into English and 14 other languages. Her main themes are liberation and women's rights, themes that derive from her own life as well as her roles as wife and mother. Listen to her read her poem "Mother's Day" at **http://www.pbs.org/wgbh/poetryeverywhere/zamora.html**

IDEAS FOR . . . Checking Comprehension

Ask students the following questions about the reading, or write them on the board.

What were the main ways in which Daisy Zamora learned English? How do these compare with ways you have learned English? Explain the similarities and the differences.

IDEAS FOR . . . Expansion

There are many different ways to learn a language, but students tend to think of academic courses as the main approach. There are a lot of other options for language learning. The goal is to create a bulletin board of resources. Perhaps students will find new ways to enhance their learning.

Ask the class to search online using the keywords *ways to learn a language.* Each person should try three different options and summarize each approach on a card for the notice board. Be sure to include the URL or Internet address where others can get more information.

Here are some non-academic suggestions:

- watch soap operas in the target language
- converse with native speakers via Skype
- join a language learning forum
- download free apps for your smartphone
- get free Web-based tools to suit your needs
- read magazines about your hobby

Understanding the Reading *(pages 129–131)*

45 mins

Check students' predictions in exercise **E** on page 123.

Answer Key

b. a personal essay

Before proceeding with the comprehension questions, ask the class if there were areas of the reading that they didn't understand. Write the letters of the paragraphs or problematic vocabulary on the board and return to them if they are not clarified in the comprehension activities.

Exercise A. | Identifying Main Ideas

- Ask students to read the questions. If necessary, have them look back at the passage and reread the relevant paragraphs. Note: Descriptions may be found in two paragraphs.
- Check the answers as a class and ask students to explain their choices by referring to lettered paragraphs in the text.

Answer Key

1. F/G **2.** I/J **3.** A/B **4.** C/D **5.** B **6.** H

Exercise B. | Identifying Key Details

- Allow time for students to write their answers individually.
- After students complete the exercise, check answers as a class. Invite volunteers to say where they found the answers to the items.

Answer Key

1. b. **2.** d **3.** c **4.** e **5.** a

CT Focus: Inferring an Author's Attitude

Go over the information in the **CT Focus** box. Often an author's attitude or feelings can be inferred from the descriptive language s/he uses.

Exercise C. | Critical Thinking: Inferring an Author's Attitude

- Students focus on four areas of the reading passage, analyzing the figurative or sensory language used in the description.
- Then, working with a partner, students discuss what the texts mean, giving examples of the way feelings are implied if not directly stated.
- Compare responses as a class, asking students to support their ideas with examples.

NOTE: Throughout this teacher's guide, letters in brackets are used to indicate the paragraph where the answer is found.

Answer Key

Answers will vary, but here are some suggestions:

1. Described as magical, mysterious; compared to strange, exotic music from faraway places; she is fascinated and excited by the differences. [A] Later, [B], she compares her grandmother's English to a bird's trill, a flute, or a dense, thick sound.
2. School English is uninspiring and mechanical, compared to shoes crunching in the gravel of the schoolyard or a cart moving over cobbled streets. She says it lacks charm, is tiresome, and repetitious. [B/C]
3. She describes it in positive terms: idyllic, beautiful, comfortable, gorgeous, peaceful, and compares it to a fairy tale. She remembers it nostalgically. [I]
4. She says it was strange, unintelligible. Her cousin calls her a weirdo and compares her to the Greek philosopher Socrates. She was frustrated, desolate, felt excluded. [J/K]

Exercise D. | Identifying Meaning from Context

- Encourage students to find the words or expressions and guess what they mean in the context of the lettered paragraph. Only then should they return to the page and complete the sentences.
- Students might want to create new sentences using these items for their vocabulary notebook.

Answer Key

1. f 2. d 3. b 4. e 5. g 6. a 7. h 8. c

Exercise E. | Critical Thinking: Analyzing Types of Language

- The goal of the exercise is to make students aware that there are different varieties and registers of language.
- Language changes rapidly, especially with technology such as texting, but also with social networking and exposure to films, television, and other media.
- Printed language—such as literature and textbooks—is often more formal than everyday teenage communication and tends to avoid current usages that may be dated and obsolete by the time the material is printed.
- Slang used by one group—whether teenagers, construction workers, or jazz musicians—has "in" words and idioms that define who is in the group and who is excluded.

Answer Key

Answers will vary according to students' own use of jargon and informal speech. In paragraph J, Zamora's cousin describes her as a "weirdo," someone outside the acceptable range of speech of her peers.

> **TIP** You may want to introduce some language that was used generations ago to make the point that language is ever-changing. With a search engine, use the keyword *slang* and the decade you are looking for (e.g., *slang 1980s*).

Exercise F. | Personalizing

Students relate Zamora's experiences to their own lives, so answers will vary.

45 mins

Developing Reading Skills
(page 132)

Reading Skill: Understanding Verbal Phrases

Writers use verbal phrases to make their writing more fluent and less choppy. A verbal is a verb form (present or past participle or infinitive) used as another part of speech. Verbal phrases are often separated from the rest of the sentence with commas for clarity.

Exercise A. | Analyzing

- Students identify the verbal phrase(s) and explain what they describe.

- It may be necessary for students to find the sentences in the reading passage to identify what is being described.

Answer Key

1. The verbal phrase [D]: *shouting their heads off with the phrase "The sky is falling, the sky is falling!"* describes cartoon characters.
2. The first verbal phrase: *transforming it into a beautiful language that kept growing inside* describes English learned at school; the second and third verbal phrases—*becoming more and more a part of my consciousness, invading my thoughts and appearing in my dreams*—describe a beautiful language. [F]
3. The three verbal phrases—*trying to understand what was being said around me, trying to decipher everything I misunderstood, assuming one thing for another*—all describe "I," the writer.
4. The verbal phrase *To be accepted by everybody* gives a reason.

IDEAS FOR... Expansion

Several TED talks explore aspects of language related to this unit's theme.

ShaoLan Hsueh, a former tech writer, investor, and entrepreneur, focuses on learning Chinese through only eight characters **http://www.ted.com/talks/shaolan_learn_to_read_chinese_with_ease.html**

Linguist John McWhorter says that texting is "fingered speech" where you write the way you talk in his "Txtng is killing language. JK!!!" at **http://www.ted.com/talks/john_mcwhorter_txtng_is_killing_language_jk.html**

JK means "just kidding" in texting.

30 mins

Viewing: Kenyans in New York *(page 133)*

Overview of the Video

Two young Kenyan men are visiting New York City for the first time and are surprised by things such as tall apartment buildings, ATM machines, people eating snack food, and hot dogs. Their guide, a New York City resident, takes all these things for granted and is not sure how to explain them.

Background Note

In recent years, male and female Kenyan athletes have won most of the major marathons or distance running races in the United States. The two young men in the video are in New York in preparation for the annual marathon. Kenyans typically train for years running at high altitudes, which gives them extra strength and stamina. Now runners from all over the world go to Kenya to train before major races.

Masai tribesmen in East Africa, such as the fit men featured in the video, go through a physically challenging period as young men to become warriors. They protect their herds of cattle from wild animals—lions, cheetahs, hyenas—on the Serengeti plain. They wear bright red plaid cloaks and are armed only with spears.

Before Viewing

Exercise A. | Using a Dictionary

- Have students work individually to match the words and their definitions.
- Compare the answers as a class.
- Ask students to predict how these words will be used in the video.

Answer Key

1. graze like cows 2. stretch (our) legs 3. grab (something)

Exercise B. | Thinking Ahead

Traveling from a small, rural community to a big city can be a huge change, even within the same country. Overall, the scale of a city—the huge buildings, the crowds, the noise, all the signs, everything going on at such a fast pace—can overwhelm a person. Answers will vary.

While Viewing

- Ask students to read the questions so they are prepared to watch and listen for certain information. They should underline the key information in each question.
- Play the video while students write short answers to the questions.
- If necessary, play the video again, pausing it at each relevant item.

Exercise A.

The first exercise is a check on prediction. What kinds of things did students predict would be issues? Which ones actually were surprising?

Exercise B.

Students read the questions and think about the answers as they watch the video.

After Viewing

Exercise A.

Pairs of students discuss their answers.

Answer Key

1. high rise apartment buildings, ATMs, people eating on the street, hot dogs
2. The *dollar* was important, as was *hot dog.*
3. In Kenya, the men traded a goat for money.
4. It depends upon the hometown, but even a small town might be surprising.

Exercise B. | Critical Thinking: Synthesizing

While the experience of New York City was an extreme contrast for the Kenyan men, they probably had a pretty good idea of what to expect, an idea shaped by exposure to the media. On the other hand, Daisy Zamora studied English for years and had very high expectations about her ability to communicate in the language, so in some ways she may have had more difficulty adjusting to the reality of a teenage subculture that she didn't expect.

IDEAS FOR . . . Expansion

Another short National Geographic video shows the two Kenyan runners training in Central Park where they meet several local residents. One man talks about his tattoos, and a homeless man describes how he lives outdoors in the park. The Kenyans show him how to make a fire with two sticks, and he is amazed. See the video at **http://channel.nationalgeographic.com/channel/videos/kenya-comes-to-central-park/**

Exploring Written English

(page 134–136)

45 mins

- Read aloud the writing goal. Personal opinion essays can take many forms—from a letter to the editor to an online blog. In this case, students will give their opinion about the best way to learn a language.

- Remind students that writing is a process. Just as there are stages of reading or viewing that lead to comprehension, there are stages in the writing process that lead to producing a final draft. The lesson starts with a review of language for writing and then presents the steps in the writing process.

- This is a good opportunity to remind students about the Independent Student Handbook at the back of their Student Book. Pages 246–248 have useful tips on academic writing and research.

Language for Writing: Adding Information with Verbal Phrases

- Go over the information and examples in the **Language for Writing** box.

- Remind students that *verbals* are verb forms that act as another part of speech within a sentence. Verb phrases start with a *verbal*—typically in its participial, gerund (*-ing*), or infinitive form—that modifies another part of the sentence.

- In exercise **A**, students choose the correct form to complete the sentence.

Exercise A.

> #### Answer Key
>
> **1.** To teach **2.** Excited **3.** Looking **4.** To increase

Exercise B. | Analyzing

Using the features described in the **Writing Skill** box, students analyze an introduction and conclusion to identify the component parts.

> ## Answer Key
>
> **Introduction:** The first sentence supplies the quotation (c.), the second sentence follows with more general information (b.), and the third sentence is the thesis statement (a.).
>
> **Conclusion:** The thesis is restated in the second sentence (d.). The following sentences elaborate on these points and the penultimate or next-to-last sentence brings the points together (e.). The final sentence offers a final thought in the form of a provocative question (f.).

Writing Skill: Writing Introductions and Conclusions

- Have students read the information in the box.

- The skill description summarizes the expected contents of the introduction and conclusion of the opinion essay.

Exercise C. | Brainstorming

- Students are directed back to the pre-reading section (exercise **D** on page 123) where they engaged in brainstorming about learning vocabulary or phrases in a new language.

- If students explored the Ideas for Expansion on page 52 of this Teacher's Guide, that may also give them material to use in this section. In addition, some of the techniques mentioned by Zamora in the reading passage may be helpful.

- Students identify three methods and support them with examples before discussing them with a partner.

Exercise D. | Vocabulary for Writing

- This section contains ways to introduce either a general point of view or a personal opinion, and students sort the phrases into these two categories.

- Check answers as a class, asking students to say why they decided a phrase was personal or general.

Writing Task: Drafting

(page 137)

Exercise A. | Planning

- This planning chart is a useful way to organize ideas before writing.

- Go over the five steps in the exercise.

- Point out that complete sentences are not necessary for the details and notes in the planning chart. The important thing is to get some ideas down on paper.

- Allow time for students to complete their charts, using ideas from exercise **C** (Brainstorming) as appropriate.

Exercise B. | Draft 1

- As students write their first draft, walk around and offer help as needed. It is not necessary to correct grammar at this stage.

- You may want to set this task for homework.

Writing Task: Revising

(pages 138–139)

Exercise C. | Critical Thinking: Analyzing

- Explain that analyzing this model essay will help students to revise their own writing.

- Allow time for students to work in pairs.

- Ask students for their opinions about what they liked or disliked in this essay.

Exercise D. | Revising

Explain that these steps will help students to reread their work carefully and look for ways to improve it.

Exercise E. | Peer Evaluation

- Explain that this process will help students to see if they have organized their ideas clearly.

- Discuss the four steps in the evaluation process to make sure students know what to do.

- Ensure that both members of the pair have equal time to give feedback.

Writing Task: Editing
(page 140)

Exercise F. | Draft 2

Walk around and monitor students as they work. Provide assistance as needed.

Exercise G. | Editing Practice

- Go over the information in the box.
- Allow time for students to find and correct the mistakes.
- Invite volunteers to write the corrected sentences on the board.

Answer Key

1. a. Taking classes every night, I learned a lot quickly.
2. b. You can take private lessons to learn a new language.
3. c. Living in a bilingual household, I learned Spanish easily.
4. c. To improve your pronunciation, you have to practice.
5. a. Watching TV in English, I learned a lot of natural language.

Exercise H. | Editing Checklist

- Read aloud the sentences in the editing checklist.
- Allow time for students to read and edit their work.

Exercise I. | Final Draft

- Allow time for students to work on their final draft (or set this for homework).
- Collect students' work.
- Let them know when they can expect to get their essays back. At that time, be sure to go over the marking system that you use.

> **IDEAS FOR . . . Follow Up**
>
> After students finish their essays, survey the class to learn what methods students favored. Can you adjust classes to include some of these methods? Is it possible to set aside time for students to do demonstration lessons of methods they like?

Resources and Development

Academic Track
History/Economics

Academic Pathways:
Lesson A: Identifying a writer's point of view
          Understanding cohesion (II)
Lesson B: Researching and note-taking
          Writing an expository essay

Unit Theme

Unit 7 explores development by examining the case of Africa, a continent with great diversity and promise that has been plagued by wars, poverty, and disease. The main reading passage argues that Africa's geography and history are the root causes of its problems, but that Africa's difficulties can be overcome.

5 mins

Think and Discuss *(page 141)*

- Ask students to describe the photo. Ask: *What is the woman carrying?* (a solar light) *Why is she carrying the light?* (In East Africa, hyenas attack other animals and people at night, so the light will scare the animals away and protect her.) *Why doesn't she just turn on other lights?* (It is likely that she doesn't have electricity or that it is too expensive. Solar energy can recharge the battery of her light during the day for free.)

- Discuss the economic base for the woman. Ask: *What kinds of conditions does she live in? How does she survive?* (The background of the photo is hazy, but it appears to be a farm with some goats. Similar to the two Kenyan men in the Unit 6 video, the woman survives by agriculture, especially herding animals and trading their milk and skins in the market for items she cannot produce. Her solar light helps to protect her herd of goats from hyena attacks.)

- Note the woman's jewelry. Ask: *Why does she have so many keys around her neck?* (Perhaps they are for vehicles or for locked sections of her farm.)

- Brainstorm possible answers to question 1 and write responses on the board. People need food to survive, so some way of getting (hunting and gathering) or producing (agriculture) food is essential. Fertile land, rainfall, and a good climate make food production easier. Next, a country needs raw materials that are valued in other places. These raw materials can be sold and exported to places where they will be processed. Gradually, a

developing country starts to process the materials domestically, thus increasing their value. As manufacturing develops, so does trade and the development of the economy.

- Answers to the second question will vary by country. Ask: *What are the main exports and imports in your country? Who are the major trade partners and why?*

- Discuss the meaning of the unit title and how it might relate to the photo. The title assumes that countries trade valuable resources as a basis for development.

15 mins

Exploring the Theme
(pages 142–143)

The opening spread features a world map coded for population density and economic development based on annual gross national income per person. This statistic is found by dividing a country's total value of goods and services by the number of people who live there. Directly below the map is a key, color-coded by one of four levels of per capita income. The lowest level is yellow, the second level is pinkish red, the third level lilac, and the fourth level blue. The most densely populated places have deeper concentrations of color.

- Allow time for students to examine the map individually, paying special attention to the keys and labels.

- Go over the map together as a class to ensure that all students know how to interpret it. Ask: *What areas are sparsely or lightly populated? How can you tell?* (There's not much color in Canada, the Amazon, Greenland, Siberia, Australia, and the Sahara.) *What cities are identified? How large are they?* (Named cities have a population of 10 million people or more.)

- Have students work with a partner to find answers to the questions in Part A.

- Discuss question 2. Note that a predominant color does not mean that everyone in that country has the same economic status. In countries with huge populations such as India and China, the average income figures disguise the extremes of wealth or poverty.

- Discuss the questions in Part B after students have read the section on defining development. Ask for examples of countries at different stages of development.

Vocabulary Notes

An *underdeveloped* country has a low standard of living (health, education, mortality, etc.) and has yet to develop industry. Agriculture is still mostly subsistence farming, and basic infrastructure such as roads, electricity, communications, and a clean water supply are still rudimentary.

Answer Key

Possible answers:

A. 1. low income: sub-Sahara and East Africa, Madagascar, Afghanistan, Myanmar, Cambodia
high income: United States and Canada, Europe, Japan, South Korea, Australia, and New Zealand
2. They have a wide range of incomes. When averaged over their large populations, they are low.
B. 1. The shift from traditional agricultural-based economies to diversified economies based on technology.
2. A developing country exports raw materials and still depends heavily on agriculture. Developed countries have more diverse economies.
3. Gross national income (GNI) per capita is one measure of a country's development.

IDEAS FOR ... Expansion

In 2000, all the countries of the United Nations agreed to eight international development goals that they hoped to achieve by 2015. The goals are relieving extreme poverty and hunger; providing primary education for all; promoting gender equality; reducing child mortality; improving maternal health; combating HIV/AIDS, malaria, and other diseases; working towards environmental sustainability; and creating a global partnership for development. Have students search for *Millennium Development Goals* (MDGs) to learn what progress has been made towards these objectives. It might be useful to use the information to prepare a display for the school or college to raise awareness.

Preparing to Read

30 mins

(pages 144–145)

WARM-UP

Some target vocabulary is presented in the context of a description of women entrepreneurs in the field of solar energy in Uganda.

In many developing countries, *microcredit,* or very small loans, is given to help poor people start small businesses. Recipients put peer pressure on each other to pay back the money, so the quality of life for everyone improves. The most famous example is the Grameen Bank in Bangladesh, which won a Nobel Prize for its work with rural poor women.

Exercise A. | Building Vocabulary

- Have students find the words in blue in the reading and use the other words around them to guess their meanings.

- Remind students that looking at the part of speech can help them figure out the meaning. Clues from surrounding words identify the part of speech. For example, *distinct, rudimentary,* and *annual* all modify nouns, so they are adjectives.

- *Thereby* is another way of saying "as a result" or "consequently" when something happens because of something else.
- Allow time for students to complete the exercise individually.

Vocabulary Notes

Rudimentary refers to the most basic or earliest stages of something. It is used for something that is elementary and not very developed. *Pete is a rudimentary musician. So far, he can only play six notes on his trumpet, but he knows four songs.*

Answer Key

1. annual
2. distinct
3. investment
4. revenue
5. rudimentary
6. thereby

Exercise B. | Building Vocabulary

- Students complete the sentences with words from the box. Encourage them to try matching words using the context before looking words up in a dictionary.
- Compare answers as a class.

Answer Key

1. orientation
2. Military intervention
3. denied
4. Evolutionary
5. Tensions
6. minority

Exercise C. | Using Vocabulary

- Ask students to think about answers to the questions before talking with a partner about them.
- Ask pairs to share their responses with the class.
- Note that answers will vary according to personal information and opinions.

Word Partners

Tension literally means to be stretched tight, but figuratively it means mental or emotional strain and stress. Sources of tension can be conflict or mistrust between countries, ethnic groups, or even individuals. Diplomats and counselors try to ease or relieve tension before all-out conflict occurs.

Exercise D. | Brainstorming

- Have students work in small groups to say what they know about Africa. Each group should have a scribe who writes down the ideas.
- Regroup the class and ask for five ideas from each group with no repetitions of what people have said before. Write the ideas on the board.
- After the class has done the reading, come back to the ideas and see which ones were relevant.

Answer Key

Answers will vary, so here are some possible responses: Geographical information such as the names of regions, countries, rivers, mountain ranges; Types of plants or animals found in Africa; Examples from Africa's history; The names of famous Africans; Problems in Africa.

Exercise E. | Predicting

- Students look at the satellite image of Africa and then read the first and last sentences of each paragraph of the passage.
- Students think of answers and discuss them with a partner.
- Check answers *after* students read the passage.

 track **2-02** You may want to play the audio while students read. Remind students that the vocabulary definitions in the numbered footnotes at the bottom of pages will help them understand the reading.

Overview of the Reading

Jared Diamond contends that geography and history are the major shaping factors in Africa. His expository article uses history and geography to explain why Africa had a different developmental path than other places and why it faces certain serious problems today. While acknowledging the issues, Diamond is optimistic that Africa can have a bright future if international investors eradicate disease and foster technological development.

Author Jared Diamond is a *polymath,* a person who is accomplished or an expert in a number of fields. Although his Ph.D. is in physiology, he is Professor of Geography at UCLA. Some of the other fields in which he is well-versed are ornithology, ecology, environmental history, and anthropology. This wide breadth of knowledge enables Diamond to investigate scientific topics in an interdisciplinary fashion and draw examples from a wide range of sources. In addition, Diamond has done field research on almost every continent, with 22 expeditions to New Guinea alone.

Diamond has authored many books, but is best known for *Guns, Germs, and Steel: The Fates of Human Societies,* which won a Pulitzer Prize, and *Collapse: How Societies Choose to Fail or Succeed,* which was the basis of a documentary series by National Geographic. Among other awards, Diamond received a MacArthur Foundation Fellowship, also known as a Genius Award.

The original Diamond article appeared in *National Geographic* in September 2005. For the source, see **http://ngm.nationalgeographic.com/ngm/0509/ resources_geo2.html**

IDEAS FOR . . . Checking Comprehension

Ask: *What are some unique things about Africa's history and role in the world?*

To what extent does geography determine how a region can develop? For example, have the world's great civilizations developed in tropical or temperate places? Why does this matter?

IDEAS FOR . . . Expansion

Learn more about the UN's Millennium Development Goals as they apply to Africa at the UN Development Program's site at **http://www.africa.undp.org/ content/rba/en/home/mdgoverview/**

Bono, the lead singer of the rock group U2, has supported anti-poverty programs in Africa for years. Learn about his fight for social justice to end poverty and disease at **http://www.ted.com/talks/bono_ the_good_news_on_poverty_yes_there_s_good_ news.html**

Understanding the Reading

45 mins *(pages 152–154)*

Check students' predictions in exercise **E** on page 145.

Answer Key

1. There is a thin temperate zone in North Africa along the Mediterranean Sea and another in South Africa, but the bulk of the continent is tropical. Moreover, the Sahara Desert covers about a third of the landmass. [B] The geographical orientation is north south. [F]
2. both history and geography **3.** both problems and solutions

Before proceeding with the comprehension questions, ask the class if there were areas of the reading that they didn't understand. Write the letters of the paragraphs or problematic vocabulary on the board and return to them if they are not clarified in the comprehension activities.

Exercise A. | Identifying Main Ideas

- Ask students to read the questions and then quickly skim the identified paragraphs to match main ideas.
- Check the answers as a class, asking students to explain their choices.

Answer Key

1. H **2.** C **3.** F **4.** D **5.** B **6.** E **7.** G

Exercise B. | Identifying Main Ideas

- Allow time for students to scan the reading for the information.
- Note that the latter three questions give practice in paraphrasing, recycled from Unit 4.

Answer Key

1. diseases **2.** temperate zones **3.** resources **4.** Public health programs can improve the health of the population, which will also have a positive effect on economies. **5.** Africa can use technology and its large English-speaking population to take part in the global economy. **6.** Outside investment to improve health and encourage development will be more effective than military intervention.

Exercise C. | Critical Thinking: Identifying Chronology

- Students use a timeline to organize the sequence of events described in paragraph C.

- In taxonomy, *genus* is a more encompassing term than *species.* Members of a species can interbreed and produce viable offspring. In the case of humans, *Homo* is the genus name and modern humans have the species name *sapiens.* Earlier humans had the species name *erectus* because of their upright posture.

Answer Key

The order from left to right is: c, d, b, a, f, e

IDEAS FOR . . . **Expansion**

Students who want to learn more about the history of mankind can visit National Geographic's Genographic project. Scientists use genetic markers to infer migration routes out of Africa. For an interactive map about these routes, see **https://genographic .nationalgeographic.com/human-journey/**

Exercise D. | Identifying Key Details

- Students seek answers to the eight questions that cover the essential content of the reading passage.

- After students complete the exercise, check answers as a class, noting the paragraph(s) where they found answers to the items.

NOTE: Throughout this teacher's guide, letters in brackets are used to indicate the paragraph where the answer is found.

Answer Key

1. Humans developed in Africa and moved outward in several migrations. [C]
2. permanent settlement, occupational specialization, population increase, civilization [E]
3. Animals and plants found there were not suitable for domestication. Also, the continent's north-south orientation impeded the spread of plants and animals because they would have to adapt to different latitudes (not such a problem with west-east diffusion). [F and G]
4. They developed a fear of humans and avoided them. [H]
5. Diseases spread more quickly from great apes and monkeys to humans because they require less adaptation. [I]
6. Much of Africa is tropical instead of temperate (more suitable for agriculture), and a third of the continent is landlocked without rivers for transport. [J]
7. He says Africa's resources are abundant and give it great potential. [K]
8. Continue to invest in public health measures to control disease, combat corruption, and use technology to be part of the global economy. [L and M]

Exercise E. | Identifying Meaning from Context

- Encourage students to find the words or expressions and guess what they mean in the context of that paragraph. Only then should they return to the page and select the closest meaning match.

- Students might want to create new sentences using these items for their vocabulary notebook.

Answer Key

1. d **2.** e **3.** h **4.** b **5.** c **6.** g **7.** a **8.** f

Vocabulary Notes

Students encountered the word *plague* before in the Unit 5 video on locusts. There it meant a widespread problem or disaster such as the swarms of insects that ate crops. In this unit, *plague* is used as a verb to indicate something that continually causes difficulty or severe problems such as the diseases and corruption in Africa.

CT Focus: Identifying Point of View

Go over the information in the **CT Focus** box. A writer's perspective is often indicated by tone, as discussed in Unit 4. In addition to examining how the author presents ideas and uses language, the overall sense of the passage is also important. Diamond is factual and realistic, but presents an optimistic, positive sense that Africa can overcome its problems.

Exercise F. | Critical Thinking: Analyzing a Writer's Point of View

The exercise gives guided practice in identifying indications of Diamond's point of view.

Answer Key

1. He wants to answer the question of whether Africa is doomed with reasons for hope. [K]
2. He cites an abundance of resources such as rivers for hydroelectric power, large animals for ecotourism, and forests that could be managed sustainably. He uses the word *harmoniously*. [K]
3. He uses *abundance,* meaning a very large quantity or extremely plentiful. It's more positive than *a lot of.* [K]
4. He is upbeat; you know this by the words he uses: *lucrative, greatly alleviated, successfully curbed,* for example. [K–M]
5. He is optimistic.

 # Developing Reading Skills

45 mins *(page 155)*

Reading Skill: Understanding Cohesion (II)

Go over the information in the **Reading Skill** box, noting the importance of key words and synonyms used for paraphrasing.

Exercise A. | Analyzing

Students scan the reading passage to find repeated use of the words *history* and *geography* or similar terms.

Answer Key

1. geography and history [B]
2. Many examples reinforce the thesis statement: *human history* in the first sentence of [C], *geography and history* in the last sentence of [D], the use of *10,000 years ago* for history in [E], *Africa's geography* in the middle of [F], *history* in the middle of [G], *the long presence* for history in [H] and again in [I], and *history and geography* in the first sentence of [J].

Exercise B. | Critical Thinking: Evaluating

Students discuss the use of repeated or paraphrased key words and give their opinions about how these devices worked in their comprehension of the reading.

IDEAS FOR . . . Expansion

Students may be interested in listening to a TED talk by Jared Diamond to see if he organizes spoken thoughts as he does his written ones. To hear his views on why societies collapse, go to **http://www.ted.com/talks/jared_diamond_on_why_societies_collapse.html**

Public broadcasting did a series on Diamond's book *Guns, Germs and Steel,* and full transcripts are available at **http://www.pbs.org/gunsgermssteel/**

Viewing: The Encroaching Desert *(page 156)*

30 mins

Overview of the Video

The video addresses the problem of *desertification*, the drying up of formerly fertile areas so that they become desert. This is a worldwide problem, but especially acute in the Sahel, the area south of the Sahara Desert. The video attributes desertification to human agricultural activity that makes the land over-used and sterile.

Background Note

The Sahel (pronounced Sah HELL) is a transitional zone between the Sahara Desert in North Africa and the savanna and tropical forests to the south. It extends from Senegal on the Atlantic coast eastward to the Sudan on the Indian Ocean. In the past, this semi-arid zone received annual monsoon rains, but cattle grazing and cutting wood for fires have increased the aridity since the 1960s. Drought and famine have increased tensions in the area between people of different ethnic and religious backgrounds. Governments in the Sahel region are unable to cope with the ecological problems and conflicts. Outside agencies, including the UN, have provided help, but once the desertification process starts, it is hard to reverse.

Before Viewing

Exercise A. | Using a Dictionary

- Have students work individually to match the words and their definitions.
- Compare the answers as a class.

Answer Key

1. sterile **2.** hectare **3.** nomadic **4.** monsoon

Vocabulary Notes

Nomadic people move from place to place during the year, often following seasonal cycles of moisture. In the past, inhabitants of the Sahel were mostly nomadic herders who moved their animals to graze where grass was available. Nomadic herders had less impact on the Sahel than sedentary farmers, so the crisis started when nomads settled in permanent villages.

Exercise B. | Thinking Ahead

A definition of desertification is given on student book page 3. The key elements are that the process is largely a result of human activities such as grazing or over cultivation.

While Viewing

- Ask students to read the questions so they are prepared to watch and listen for certain information. They should underline the key information in each question.
- Play the video while students write short answers to the questions.

After Viewing

Exercise A.

- Have students work in pairs to discuss and compare answers.
- Ask students if there are any points that are unclear that they wish to discuss.

Answer Key

1. a fertile region
2. They watered wild vegetation that protected the soil from drought and eroding winds.
3. According to the video, on all continents.
4. It is turning into desert.

Exercise B. | Critical Thinking: Synthesizing

In his book *Collapse: How Societies Choose to Fail or Succeed,* Diamond explains how habitat destruction and soil problems have contributed to the failure of societies in the past and will again if people ignore the natural carrying capacity of the land.

Exploring Written English
(pages 157–160)

45 mins

- Read aloud the writing goal. Expository essays describe or explain something. Following the lead of Jared Diamond, students will write about how a country has been affected by its history or geography.

- Remind students that writing is a process. Just as there are stages of reading or viewing that lead to comprehension, there are stages in the writing process that lead to producing a final draft. The lesson reviews language for writing and then presents the steps in the writing process.

- Remind students about the Independent Student Handbook at the back of their Student Book. Pages 246–248 have useful tips on academic writing and research. Page 250 has a list of verbs and phrases often used in expository writing.

Exercise A. | Brainstorming

- Students think of three places—regions or countries—that have been affected by their history or geography.

- The goal is to activate background knowledge about different places so that one can be selected as the focus of the expository essay.

Exercise B. | Vocabulary for Writing

- Have students locate the words in the lettered paragraphs of the main reading and guess their meanings from context before using the words to complete the sentences.

- Check answers as a class, asking students to use each word in a new sentence.

Answer Key

1. d 2. a 3. b 4. f 5. c 6. e

Free Writing

- Remind students that free writing is writing rapidly to come up with ideas without worrying about mistakes.

- Set a time limit of five minutes for students to free write about one historical or geographic aspect of the region or country they chose in exercise **A.** Encourage students to use vocabulary from exercise **B.**

Exercise C.

- In academic writing, it is important to accurately cite writers of source material by using direct quotes or by paraphrasing. The **Language for Writing** box

demonstrates how reporting verbs are used to refer to sources.

- The exercise provides practice in reporting material from the reading passage using both quotes and paraphrases.

Answer Key

Answers will vary, but here are some possibilities:

1. According to Diamond, "the first humans they encountered were already fully modern people, with modern brains and hunting skills."
2. Diamond says, "I've been struck by how harmoniously ethnic groups live together in many countries—far better than they do in many other parts of the globe."
3. Diamond argues that improving public health is a good investment because it improves the economy, too.
4. Diamond believes that technology will link Africa to the rest of the world.

IDEAS FOR . . . Further Research

If students would like further practice in referring to sources, a transcript of questions Diamond answered in an interview with UCLA is available online. See the site at **http://today.ucla.edu/portal/ut/10-questions-jared-diamond-collapse-171817.aspx**

Writing Skill: Researching and Note-taking

- Have students read the information in the box, highlighting things they will do differently.

- Have a class discussion about techniques students use to take notes, focusing on taking clear, accurate electronic notes.

Exercise D. | Critical Thinking: Researching

After pairs of students have discussed the questions, ask for volunteers to tell about their key words and Web sites.

Answer Key

Answers will vary, but possibilities are:

1. agricultural production Africa
2. African spoken languages
3. foreign aid to Africa

Many international Web sites would be good resources including the UN Development Program, NGOs (non-government organizations), and academic sites. Hint: For African spoken languages, add images to the search for many distribution maps.

Exercise E. | Critical Thinking: Note-Taking

Students read two sets of notes and decide which is better.

Answer Key

Example "a" is superior because it contains more details from the original. The other example is too condensed and thus loses some of its meaning.

Exercise F. | Critical Thinking: Applying

Students research the region or country they identified before. They look for geographical and historical information that apply to its current situation.

Answer Key

Answers will vary with the country or region chosen. As an example, the desertification of the area around the Aral Sea was mentioned in the video. If Uzbekistan—where most of the sea is located—were chosen as a topic, it would be important to note that it is a landlocked country that in the past used the Aral Sea for fishing. During the Soviet regime, the government decided to promote the production of cotton for the world market and thus used water from two of the rivers (the Amu Darya and the Syr Darya) that feed the Aral Sea. Consequently, the body of water is now only 10 percent of its original size. In addition, the area around the sea is very polluted, resulting in health problems for inhabitants. Moreover, the loss of the large body of water has had an effect on the climate, making the region drier and creating dust storms. Geography, history, and human impact have all had an effect on the decline of the Aral Sea.

Writing Task: Drafting

(page 161)

Exercise A. | Planning

- Point out that this planning chart is a useful way to organize ideas before writing.

- Go over the four steps in the exercise, noting that there will be an introduction, three body paragraphs, and a conclusion.

- Point out that complete sentences are not necessary for the details and notes in the planning chart. The important thing is to get some ideas down on paper.

- Allow time for students to complete their charts.

Exercise B. | Draft 1

Remind students that the purpose of a first draft is to get ideas down on paper. They will have time to revise and edit later.

Writing Task: Revising

(pages 162–163)

Exercise C. | Critical Thinking: Analyzing

- Explain that analyzing this model essay will help students to revise their own writing.

- Encourage students to pay particular attention to how the author has treated sources and used reporting verbs.

Answer Key

1. The thesis statement is the last sentence in the first paragraph, and the key words are *geographical location, lack of natural resources,* and *recent history of immigration.*
2. The topic sentences occur as the first sentences in paragraphs 2, 3, and 4. The order reflects the order of ideas in the thesis.
3. The key words in the topic sentences—*geography, lack of natural resources,* and *recent history of immigration*—are nearly the same as in the thesis statement.
4. In paragraph 2, the water surrounding Singapore supports the geographical location. This is developed with shipping and ports.
   In paragraph 3, the lack of drinking water is detailed with the importation of water, desalination, and water recycling.
   In paragraph 4, immigration is cited as a solution to low birthrates, the need to maintain a strong workforce, and to offset an aging population.
5. In paragraph 3, the Public Utilities Board is cited (according to…), and in paragraph 4, an interview in Forbes magazine is given as the information source (Rogers argued, pointed out…).

Exercise D. | Revising

Students follow the same analytical steps as they reread their work carefully and look for ways to improve it.

Exercise E. | Peer Evaluation

- Remind students that this process will help students to see if they have organized their ideas clearly.

- Ensure that both members of the pair have equal time to give feedback.

Writing Task: Editing
(page 164)

Exercise F. | Draft 2
Walk around and monitor students as they work. Provide assistance as needed.

Exercise G. | Editing Practice
- Go over the information in the box.
- Allow time for students to find and correct the mistakes.
- Invite volunteers to write the corrected sentences on the board.

Answer Key

1. Susan Sontag said that to photograph is to confer importance.
2. According to Griffiths, photography has influenced our notion of what is beautiful.
3. Diamond asks, "What's the best case for Africa's future?"
4. As Kolbert says, "Probably the most obvious way humans are altering the planet is by building cities."

Exercise H. | Editing Checklist
- Read aloud the sentences in the editing checklist.
- Allow time for students to read and edit their work.

Exercise I. | Final Draft
- Allow time for students to work on their final draft (or set this for homework).
- Collect students' work.
- Let them know when they can expect to get their essays back. At that time, be sure to go over the marking system that you use.

IDEAS FOR . . . Further Research
If students want to learn more about development, a well-regarded academic site with many links is Wellesley College's Development Studies Internet Resources at **http://academics.wellesley.edu/Polisci/wj/DevelopmentLinks/development-links.htm**

Living Longer

Academic Track
Health and Medicine

Academic Pathways:

Lesson A: Predicting a conclusion
Asking questions as you read

Lesson B: Planning a research paper
Writing an argumentative
research paper

Unit Theme

Unit 8 explores the issue of longevity, focusing especially on societies where a disproportionate number of people live healthy lives into their 90s and beyond. The readings and video describe recent research with very old people that analyzes factors that seem to contribute to long lives.

Think and Discuss *(page 165)*

5 mins

- Ask students to describe the photo. Ask: *What do you see in the photo? Why is the man showing his arm? What does a person have to do to get large muscles?*

- The photograph shows an 89-year-old fisherman from Okinawa, an archipelago or group of islands off Japan. It is likely that the man is still actively engaged in fishing and has developed muscles in the course of his work. Most people who live to age 89 are no longer working or physically active. The man's facial expression indicates that he is pleased with himself that he is so fit.

- Discuss possible answers to questions 1 and 2. The questions are subjective, so individual responses may differ. Ask about healthy parts of a daily routine. Regular exercise, eating a nutritious diet, and not smoking are fundamental. Less obvious factors are keeping up an active face-to-face social life, continuing to work or making a contribution to the community, and staying mentally stimulated.

- In response to question 2, genetic heritage clearly plays a role, but it may not be as important as lifestyle issues.

- Sometimes genes can have a negative effect on longevity. For example, if a woman's female relatives have histories of breast cancer, she is more likely to develop the disease. Similarly, some forms of Alzheimer's disease seem to run in families.

- Discuss the meaning of the unit title and how it might relate to the photo. Ask students how long they would like to live and what they plan to do to make that likely.

Exploring the Theme *(pages 166–167)*

15 mins

- The opening spread features infographics from the *National Geographic Atlas, Ninth Edition,* on causes of death and the correlation between income and life expectancy.

- The world map uses color coding to show whether most deaths in a country are attributable to contagious diseases (AIDS, malaria, cholera), noncommunicable diseases (cancer, heart disease, diabetes), or injuries (accidents, murder, warfare). In general, developing countries have more fatalities from contagious diseases whereas in developed countries, noncommunicable diseases are more common causes for death.

- Draw students' attention to the triangular map key. In the atlas, the key is clearer and there are descriptions of representative countries. Note that the original key distinguishes between white for "no data available" (Greenland, Western Sahara, the Balkans) and beige for injuries (Iraq, due to warfare).

- In the atlas, Canada represents a developed country where 58 percent of all deaths result from cancer or cardiovascular problems. In Colombia, injuries from conflict (civil war and drug trade) account for 44 percent of all deaths. In Botswana, 84 percent of all deaths are due to communicable diseases such HIV/AIDS.

- Below the map, income and life expectancy are shown with bar graphs and circles contrasting levels in 1960 with 2000. Students also have access to figures for annual per capita income, similar to the gross national income measurement in Unit 7.

- Allow time for students to study the map and charts individually. Then discuss the questions together as a class.

- In discussing question 5, note that some areas grouped together have very different life expectancies and standards of living. One example is Europe grouped with Central Asia, and another is the Caribbean with Latin America. For instance, Haiti and Brazil are not comparable in annual per capita income or life expectancy.

Answer Key

Hint: It may be helpful to work with a world map labeled with country names.
Possible answers:

1. noncommunicable diseases (examples: diabetes, heart disease, and cancer)
2. Communicable diseases are prime causes of death in sub-Saharan Africa and Afghanistan. Injuries are the main cause of death in Colombia, Venezuela, Algeria, Iraq, Sri Lanka, and Indonesia.
3. Answers will vary with country.
4. Some factors are access to clean drinking water and health care, lifestyle factors (diet, exercise, habits), and income.
5. Higher income correlates positively with higher life expectancy.

IDEAS FOR ... Expansion

Ask students to research *life expectancy,* the number of years an average newborn is expected to live if the statistics at the time of birth stay the same throughout life. There are many comprehensive sources, but here are some resources to compare:

World Health Organization

http://www.who.int/whr/2004/annex/topic/en/ annex_4_en.pdf

The World Bank

http://data.worldbank.org/indicator/SP.DYN.LE00.IN

CIA figures for 2013, rank ordered from highest to lowest

https://www.cia.gov/library/publications/the-world-factbook/rankorder/2102rank.html

---

Preparing to Read

(pages 168–169)

30 mins

WARM-UP

Target vocabulary is contained within a description of how hunger works and the implications for dieting to lose weight.

Ask students about their eating habits. *How many meals a day do you eat? Do you snack between meals? When do you get hungry? Do you eat while you are studying, watching TV, or using the computer? Why or why not?*

Exercise A. | Building Vocabulary

- Have students find the words in blue in the reading and use other words around them to guess their meanings.

- Remind students that looking at the part of speech can help them figure out the meaning. Clues from surrounding words identify the part of speech. *Mechanisms, implication,* and *restriction* are all nouns. *Conversely* is related to *on the contrary* from Unit 6. Both of them introduce a contrasting idea. *Contradictory* is an adjective that describes two opposed or inconsistent ideas.

- When you *gain insight into* something, you understand a situation in a very clear way. Some insights are intuitive or emotional as well as rational. Note that the three words are always collocated.

- Allow time for students to complete the exercise individually.

Answer Key

1. contradictory
2. conversely
3. gain insight into
4. implication
5. reconstruct
6. restrictions
7. mechanism

Word Link

The Latin root *struct* has the meaning of *build*. Ask the class to explain how *build* is connected to the example words given. For instance, to *instruct* is to build knowledge, and the person who does this is an *instructor*. Students have encountered the word *infrastructure* in reading passages. It means a society's basic facilities and structures such as roads and communication links. They may also recognize *obstruction,* something that gets in the way. All of these words are built on the same root *struct.*

Exercise B. | Building Vocabulary

- Students complete the sentences with words from the box. Encourage them to try to match words with the context before looking words up in a dictionary.
- Compare answers as a class.

Answer Key

1. Unification **2.** outnumbers **3.** distinction **4.** intact
5. ratio

Word Link

The prefix *uni-* means one. Ask about these words: *unique, unicycle, unison,* and *universal.* How do they all use "one"?

Exercise C. | Using Vocabulary

- Ask students to think about answers to the questions before talking with a partner about them.
- Ask pairs to share their responses with the class.

Answer Key

Answers will vary. People have dietary restrictions for many reasons including allergies; medical, religious, and cultural reasons; and personal preference (such as vegan).

Exercise D. | Brainstorming

- Students work in groups of three or four to discuss the questions.
- This exercise is intended to activate background knowledge about longevity before students read the passage.

Answer Key

Possible answers may include genetics, lifestyle choices (diet, exercise, habits such as smoking or drinking), where people live, their socioeconomic status, access to medical care, etc.

Exercise E. | Predicting

- Have students look at the photos on pages 171–177 and skim the reading passage. Then they predict the topics that will be covered in the passage.
- Check students' answers *after* they read the passage.

Exercise F. | Critical Thinking: Predicting a Conclusion

Have students read the first three paragraphs of the reading passage.

Answer Key

1. They are trying to determine factors in longevity.
2. From the first three paragraphs, it seems likely that they discovered that lifestyle factors are important.

CT Focus: Predicting a Conclusion

Readers are encouraged to engage with the text as they read, making predictions and checking them throughout the passage.

> **IDEAS FOR . . . Expansion**
>
> A well-known graphic organizer is a **KWL** chart in which **K** stands for what a person already <u>knows</u> about a topic, **W** for what the person <u>wants</u> to learn about it, and **L** for what was <u>learned</u>. This is closely related to the CT focus of predicting a conclusion. The important thing is to use any background knowledge to interact with the text. Often, readers are surprised that they learn things they didn't predict or expect. Ask if students have used a KWL chart. If not, suggest that they try with this reading.

Developing Reading Skills
(page 170)

45 mins

Reading Skill: Asking Questions as You Read

The information in the **Reading Skills** box suggests that readers are trying to discern two things: information presented in the passage, and the author's purpose or point of view. As discussed in previous units, the author's purpose and perspective can be inferred from how the information is presented, the organization of the passage, and the vocabulary used to describe ideas.

Paragraph A mentions the professions of the two researchers, so the reader might assume that they are going to pursue their specialties. A *geneticist* is likely to take biological samples (blood, urine, buccal swabs from the cheek, etc.) to test DNA. A *geriatrician* is a physician who specializes in the process and problems of aging and therefore works with elderly patients. Today the adjective phrase "old old" is often used for people 85 years old or older.

Exercise A. | Asking Questions as You Read

The chart provides a matrix for students to pose and answer questions as they read through the article. Answers will vary individually as each student interprets the content in the paragraphs.

track 2-03 You may want to play the audio while students read. Remind students that the vocabulary definitions in the numbered footnotes at the bottom of the pages will help them understand the reading.

Overview of the Reading

The reading passage describes how an interdisciplinary team of researchers in Italy is exploring longevity from several different perspectives. They talk with centenarians about their personal histories and lifestyles, they take blood samples to process biochemically, they search through historical records to reconstruct family pedigrees, and they do DNA analysis.

Background

Longevity describes duration or length of life, especially long life into the ninth decade or more. It is sometimes confused with *life expectancy,* but—as described above—that is a statistical concept based on the likely age a newborn baby will achieve at the end of life. Researchers of longevity try to find documentary evidence (birth, government, or church records) to support claims that a person is of advanced age.

As suggested in paragraph H of the passage, longevity is a topic subject to speculation, bogus claims, and commercial exploitation. Since most people would like to live long, healthy lives, popular culture is full of tabloid articles, television programs, and advertisements that claim to have the secret to living long and well. The reading passage points out that there's no single panacea or explanation for why some people live a century or more.

The original article by Stephen Hall is at **http://ngm .nationalgeographic.com/2013/05/longevity/hall-text** and there is an interactive visual on genetic clues to a long life at **http://ngm.nationalgeographic .com/2013/05/longevity/genetic-clues-graphic**

> ### IDEAS FOR . . . Checking Comprehension
>
> Ask students the following questions about the reading, or write them on the board.
>
> *How do these Italian researchers do their work? Describe their methods. What are their specialty areas?*

Understanding the Reading
(pages 178–180)

45 mins

Check students' predictions in exercises **E** and **F** on page 169.

> ### Answer Key
>
> The text contains all items except happiness, friends, and socializing, but these three are suggested by the photographs. Two photos emphasize exercise and two others suggest that having meaningful work is important.

Before proceeding with the comprehension questions, ask the class if there were areas of the reading that they didn't understand. Write the letters of the paragraphs or problematic vocabulary on the board and return to them if they are not clarified in the comprehension activities.

Exercise A. | Understanding Main Ideas

- Ask students to read the questions. If necessary, have them look back at the passage and reread the relevant paragraphs. Note: Information may be found in two or more paragraphs.

- Check the answers as a class and ask students to explain their choices by referring to lettered paragraphs in the text.

NOTE: Throughout this teacher's guide, letters in brackets are used to indicate the paragraph(s) where the answer is found.

Answer Key

1. Calabria has an unusually high percentage of nonagenarians and centenarians as well as comprehensive demographic records dating back to 1866. Calabria's mountainous geography creates isolated villages where many people still live a traditional lifestyle. [A, H–L]
2. Scientists have learned that both genetics and environment are important, but neither factor entirely and sufficiently explains why some people live so long. They look at other factors such as chance. Specific things they've learned include the fact that in Calabria, genetics benefit males more than females, that people in their 90s and beyond have genes that enhance digestion and metabolism, and that restricting food intake does not necessarily confer longevity. [L–O, R–S]

Exercise B. | Identifying Key Details

- Allow time for students to write their answers individually before working with a partner.
- After students complete the exercise, check answers as a class. Invite volunteers to say where they found the answers to the items.

Answer Key

1. A centenarian's siblings may have similar genes, but their spouses wouldn't although they share the same lifestyle. [L]
2. They used official government records of births, marriages, and deaths going back to 1866. [I–K]
3. Very elderly people have a gene that promotes the digestion of certain green foods. Another gene makes metabolism more efficient. [N–O]
4. Studies with both mice and monkeys suggest that caloric restriction can have many effects, but does not predictably lead to longer lives. [R]

Exercise C. | Identifying Supporting Examples

Answer Key

Most of the examples are for external or lifestyle factors: Domenico's diet (*a little of everything*), Maria Rosa's singing (*about a local saint*), Salvatore's maxim (*no drinking, smoking, or women*), reading, diet (*mostly vegetarian*), men serving in the military, and women paying more attention to diet and medical care. The only genetic example is that the Calabrian study shows that genetics favor men, and the only chance factor mentioned was Salvatore breaking his leg so he didn't have to serve in the military during WWII.

Exercise D. | Identifying Meaning from Context

- Encourage students to find the words or expressions and guess what they mean in the context of the lettered paragraph.
- Students might want to create new sentences using these items for their vocabulary notebook.

Answer Key

1. b 2. c 3. e 4. d 5. g 6. a 7. f 8. i 9. h

Exercise E. | Identifying Meaning from Context

Students locate the words or expressions and guess what they mean in the context of the lettered paragraph.

Answer Key

1. b 2. d 3. a 4. e 5. c

TIP Despite two sections on identifying words from context, there are still many unfamiliar words in the reading. Suggest that students find these and create their own exercise for the class. Some suggestions (with collocations) are:

[C] *prodigiously* intact
[H] *genomic* technologies
[O] *uncoupling* protein
[P] *curtails* longevity
[Q] *plethora* of new studies

Exercise F. | Understanding Infographics

There are four aspects to the key for the diagram on page 176. One is health care spending per person, given in U.S. dollars next to the country name. Point out that countries are rank-ordered according to this number. The second aspect is the thickness of the line, which indicates the number of doctor visits per person each year. The third aspect is the color of the line—blue or red—which indicates whether a country has universal health care (everyone is covered) or not. The fourth aspect, life expectancy at birth, is on the right side of the chart in yearly units numbered every five years.

Answer Key

1. most: U.S. at $7,290; least: Mexico at $823
2. highest (12+): Japan and the Czech Republic; lowest (0–3): Switzerland, Sweden, U.S., and Mexico
3. longest: Japan (82.7 years); shortest: Hungary (73.2 years)

Exercise G. | Critical Thinking: Making Inferences

Students look for patterns in the data.

Answer Key

The chart seems to show very little relationship between spending on health care, doctor visits, and longevity (with the exception of Japan which has the longest life expectancy and a high average number of doctor visits per year).

Exercise H. | Personalizing

Students talk with a partner about living to be 100. They support their opinions with reasons.

IDEAS FOR . . . Expansion

Dan Buettner has researched longevity for *National Geographic*. A key article of his is found at **http://ngm.nationalgeographic.com/2005/11/longevity-secrets/buettner-text**

Buettner's TED talk on *How to Live to be 100* is very popular. It can be viewed at **http://www.ted.com/talks/dan_buettner_how_to_live_to_be_100.html**

Viewing: Secrets of a Long Life *(page 181)*

Overview of the Video

National Geographic photographer David McLean was part of a team that visited three places renowned for their populations of very old people who live active and healthy lives. The team visited Sardinia in southern Italy, Okinawa, Japan, and the Adventist community of Loma Linda in California. There are differences between the three communities, but they are outweighed by the similarities. In all three, older adults lead active, purposeful lives that they share with their family and friends.

Background Note

Investigation of the factors that lead to long lives is an enduring research topic. In 1919, none other than Alexander Graham Bell—the inventor of the telephone—wrote an article on the topic for National Geographic. In the 1920s, the Longevity Project was started, research that tracked 1500 individuals over the course of their lives to identify relevant factors in aging. In 2005, National Geographic partnered with Daniel Buettner and others in an interactive expedition to the Blue Zones, places where seniors live very long and active lives. Photographer McLean narrates a parallel version of the video with some different photographs at **http:// ngm.nationalgeographic.com/ngm/0511/sights_n_ sounds/index.html**.

Before Viewing

Exercise A. | Using a Dictionary

- Have students work individually to match the words and their definitions.
- Compare the answers as a class.
- Ask students to predict how these words will be used in the video.

Answer Key

1. sedentary 2. devout 3. obesity 4. unplug

Vocabulary Notes

The transcript and narration of the video differ slightly. The narration uses the phrase *"women wear the pants"* to describe Sardinian women taking charge of family finances and household management which has the effect of reducing stress on men.

The terms *vital* and *vitality* are used several times. They mean necessary, essential, and full of energy. Okinawa is in an *archipelago,* a large group or cluster of islands south of Japan.

Exercise B. | Thinking Ahead

Students work together to list habits that they think help people to live longer. As they watch the video, they note which are mentioned.

While Viewing

- Ask students to read questions 1–4 so they are prepared to watch and listen for certain information. They should underline the key information in each question.
- Play the video while students write short answers to the questions.
- If necessary, play the video again, pausing it at each relevant item.

Exercise A.

The first exercise is a check on the habits students predicted. Which were mentioned in the video? What other habits were surprising?

After Viewing

Exercise A.

Pairs of students discuss their answers.

Answer Key

1. They are all active participants in their communities, both in terms of physical activity and social interaction with people of all generations. They all eat healthy diets that are largely vegetarian and eschew bad habits.
2. As members of a religious community, the Adventists are strict vegetarians and don't drink alcohol or smoke.
3. In Sardinia and Okinawa, young people have different lifestyles.
4. For religious reasons, young people in Loma Linda continue the traditional lifestyle.

Exercise B. | Critical Thinking: Synthesizing

Students consider the reading passage and the video together.

Answer Key

1. The Italian researchers have found genetic evidence for men living long lives as well as women.
2. Although this may be a factor, more recent research indicates that caloric restriction is not as important as once thought.
3. The article—especially on the point of caloric restriction—is more recent.

IDEAS FOR . . . Expansion

Wikipedia has a useful Venn diagram that contrasts and compares the factors for longevity in Sardinia, Okinawa, and Loma Linda at **http://en.wikipedia.org/wiki/File:Vendiagram.gif**

Exploring Written English

(pages 182–184)

45 mins

- Read aloud the writing goal. Students will prepare to write an argumentative research paper about scientific research on aging.

- Remind students that writing is a process. Just as there are stages of reading or viewing that lead to comprehension, there are stages in the writing process that lead to producing a final draft. This lesson starts with evaluating material in preparation for choosing a topic, reviewing language for writing about evidence, and then going through the steps in the writing process.

Writing Skill: Planning a Research Paper

- Have students read the information in the box, highlighting the important steps involved in planning an argumentative research paper.

- Remind students about the Independent Student Handbook at the back of their Student Book. Pages 246–248 have useful tips on academic writing and research, including a helpful research checklist on page 248.

Exercise A. | Critical Thinking: Evaluating

Students mark the statements that would be good topics for an argumentative essay. Statements of fact or information—such as items 1, 4, and 6—are not good choices, but the more contentious statements (2, 3, 5) would be good topics to argue.

Exercise B. | Critical Thinking: Evaluating

- This time, students select statements that support the thesis: "Cigarette smoking around children should be made illegal." Note that this is item five from Exercise A.

- Discuss the thesis with the class so that everyone understands that the focus is adults smoking in the presence of children (secondhand smoke), not smoking in general.

- Statements 3, 4, and 7 clearly support the thesis, while item 6 applies to smokers in general. Ask the class to explain why the other statements are not appropriate for this task.

Exercise C. | Brainstorming

Remind the class that a **T-chart**—called that because of its shape—is a graphic organizer used to compare pros and cons about a subject. In this case, students brainstorm ideas that support or refute the provided topic about research on longevity.

Exercise D. | Researching and Note-taking

- Students apply their note-taking skills from Unit 7 as they research the topic. They use the T-chart again to organize new information and decide on their position for the thesis statement of their essay.

- Go over the information and examples in the **Language for Writing** box.

- Remind students that evidence does not stand on its own; the writer must show how it supports the argument. When deeply involved in researching a topic, the connections seem obvious, but the reader will not have the same background on the subject.

Exercise E. | Applying

Students demonstrate how the statements support the thesis argument.

Answer Key

Answers will vary, but here are some possibilities:

1. This demonstrates the serious risk that parental smoking poses to children.
2. This supports the idea that passive exposure to smoke can be fatal.
3. As this evidence shows, actual tobacco use kills people, but so does exposure to secondhand smoke.
4. This research shows that smoking around children has a long-term negative effect in addition to the immediate health hazard.

Writing Task: Drafting
(page 185)

Exercise A. | Planning

- This planning chart is a useful way to organize ideas before writing.
- Go over the six steps in the exercise.
- Point out that complete sentences are not necessary for the details and notes in the planning chart. The important thing is to get some ideas down on paper.
- Draw attention to the suggestion in Step 3 to locate the strongest argument in the last body paragraph.
- Allow time for students to complete their charts, using ideas from the T-chart as appropriate.

Exercise B. | Draft 1

- As students write their first draft, walk around and offer help as needed. It is not necessary to correct grammar at this stage.
- You may want to set this task for homework.

Writing Task: Revising
(pages 186–187)

Exercise C. | Critical Thinking: Analyzing

- Explain that analyzing this model essay will help students to revise their own writing.
- Allow time for students to analyze the essay individually before discussing it with a partner.
- Draw attention to the colored boxes that provide helpful suggestions on citing sources, leading in to the topic, and dealing with opposing arguments. Note that inclusion of other points of view can strengthen the credibility of an argument.
- Add a step to the process. Have students draw a line between evidence cited in the model essay and the reference list on page 187. Point out that all references were retrieved from online sources.

Answer Key

1. The thesis statement is the last sentence in the first paragraph.
2. Opposing viewpoints occur in the first paragraph (sentence starting with Right now…), second paragraph (highlighted in green), and the first sentences in the third and fifth paragraphs. In three of these cases, the opposing views form only part of the sentence.
3. The topic sentences occur as the first sentences in paragraphs 2, 3, and 4.
4. In paragraph 2, the evidence includes WHO statistics and the quote by Garbarino. In paragraph 3, the evidence is from WHO on the effect of smoke on infants. In paragraph 4, the evidence is the Schwarz article and WHO statistics. In paragraph 2, *According to the WHO statistics* and the same thing in paragraph 3. In paragraph 4, *According to an article . . . , this greatly increases,* and *These statistics combined show. . . .*
5. In the conclusion, main points are reviewed in the last two sentences (*fewer children dying from secondhand smoke, fewer children becoming smokers,* and *it would protect those who can't protect themselves*).

Exercise D. | Revising

Explain that these steps will help students to reread their work carefully and look for ways to improve it.

Exercise E. | Peer Evaluation

- Explain that this process will help students to see if they have organized their ideas clearly.
- Discuss the four steps in the evaluation process to make sure students know what to do.
- Ensure that both members of the pair have equal time to give feedback.

Writing Task: Editing
(page 188)

Exercise F. | Draft 2

Walk around and monitor students as they work. Provide assistance as needed.

Exercise G. | Editing Checklist

Allow time for students to read and edit their work.

Exercise H. | Final Draft

- Allow time for students to work on their final draft (or set this for homework).
- Collect students' work.

- Let them know when they can expect to get their essays back. At that time, be sure to go over the marking system that you use.

IDEAS FOR . . . Follow Up

Students may want to link the topics in this unit by researching the connection between *smoking and longevity* by using those two keywords in searches. There is considerable evidence that smokers who quit in midlife can boost their life span. However, because this is a highly contentious topic, students should pay attention to the type of sources they use. For example, medical or scholarly sources are more credible than blogs or popular magazines.

Memorable Experiences

Academic Track
Interdisciplinary

Academic Pathways:
Lesson A: Making inferences
Analyzing a personal narrative
Lesson B: Using sensory details
Writing an extended
personal narrative

Unit Theme

Unit 9 focuses on memorable personal experiences and the impact they have on a person's life and career.

Think and Discuss *(page 189)*

5 mins

- Ask students to describe the photo. Ask: *What do you see in the photo? What activity is going on here? Why do you think people choose to travel this way?*

- The photograph shows two young Russian hitchhikers standing by the side of a road and holding a sign for Moscow. A large freight truck is passing them. The background landscape is bleak with no indication of settlement or commercial activity.

- Discuss the idea of *hitchhiking,* traveling by asking for free rides from strangers. Travelers sometimes display a sign with their destination or at other times stick out their thumb to indicate they would like a ride. The latter has given the practice the name of "thumbing" a ride. Different gestures are used in some cultures. People primarily hitchhike as a means of free travel, so hitchhiking is most common among young people.

- In recent years, hitchhiking has raised safety concerns because sometimes either the traveler or the driver takes advantage of the situation. Consequently, some countries have outlawed hitchhiking. By contrast, it is encouraged in some places where transport is limited. Ask the class about how hitchhiking is regarded in their countries.

- Discuss possible answers to questions 1 and 2. The questions are subjective, so individual responses may differ. Start by asking for volunteers to tell about their travel experiences and why they were memorable.

- For question 2, ask whether young people are encouraged to travel and why or why not. In some places, a period of travel is seen as a "rite

of passage" for young people before they assume adult responsibilities. For example, some students use a "gap year" as a time to travel and live abroad. Sometimes hitchhiking is organized to benefit a social cause. Every spring in the U.K. and Europe, thousands of students hitchhike to Morocco, Prague, or Croatia to raise money for education in Africa. Learn more about this charitable initiative at **http://www.lcdinternational.org/hitch**

- Discuss the meaning of the unit title and how it might relate to the photo.

Exploring the Theme *(pages 190–191)*

15 mins

- The opening spread features quotations about the value of travel and meeting new people. The quotes are by famous people from all over the world, suggesting that travel is a universally broadening experience. The background photograph depicts people climbing huge sand dunes in a national park in Namibia.

- Allow time for students to study the photograph and read the quotes before opening up a class discussion.

- In discussing questions 2 and 3, ask: *Which quote(s) do you agree with and why? Which quote(s) do you disagree with? Explain why. Do you know similar quotes? As a language learner, do you have expressions from your personal experience with new cultures?*

- Ask the class what they know about the people quoted on pages 190–191. If they are not familiar with them, assign researching them as homework.

- Students might enjoy finding additional quotes and illustrating a poster with them. Useful key words for searching are *quotes about travel and education* or *inspiring travel quotes*.

Answer Key

Meanings of quotes from upper right:

Lin Yutang: Travel makes you more appreciative of home. **Moslih Eddin Saadi:** The key to experiencing a new culture is to be very aware of your surroundings. **Maya Angelou:** Travel makes us aware of what all humans share so we can connect to one another. **Freya Stark:** Travel is very personal and it can be pleasant to experience it by yourself. **Jawaharlal Nehru:** The world is an amazing place, but we have to be receptive to appreciate it. **Ibn Battuta:** Initially, a traveler is preoccupied in taking in experiences, but then s/he wants to relate them to others. **Robert Louis Stevenson:** The traveler looking outward sees the strangeness of different cultures, but it really is the traveler who is different. **William Butler Yeats:** He optimistically thinks everyone is a potential friend.

IDEAS FOR ... Expansion

Hitchhiking features prominently as a topic in popular culture such as films, TV programs, literature, and music. Have students use the guide to such resources at http://en.wikipedia.org/wiki/Hitchhiking to explore the topic further.

Preparing to Read

(pages 192–193)

30 mins

WARM-UP

Target vocabulary is contained within paragraphs about memories of events or travel. The concept of "flashbulb memory" is introduced. This is when a person has a detailed memory of a surprising and emotional event like a public tragedy.

Ask if students have "flashbulb memories" of particular events, understanding that some events might be painful to remember. For example, talking about natural disasters such as tsunamis or earthquakes could trigger bad memories.

Exercise A. | Building Vocabulary

- Have students find the words in blue in the reading and use other words around them to guess their meanings.

- Remind students that looking at the part of speech can help them figure out the meaning. Clues from surrounding words identify the part of speech. In this case, most of the target words are verbs. Ask the class to find the five verbs (*ensure, confront, transcend, expose, devise*) and the words surrounding them to say how they function in the context.

- Allow time for students to complete the exercise individually.

Answer Key

1. exposed
2. transcends
3. confronted
4. assignments
5. devise
6. massive
7. ensure

Word Usage

Native speakers often confuse *insure* and *ensure,* but the two words are not interchangeable. If you *ensure* something, you guarantee it or make certain that it happens. *To ensure my arrival at the airport on time, I left three hours early. Insure* means to protect something or someone against risk. *We insure our car against the risk of an accident.* Typically, *insure* is associated with buying *insurance.*

IDEAS FOR ... Expansion

Flashbulb memories are a form of autobiographical memories, when people vividly recall personal experiences in their life such as where they were and what they were doing when they learned some shocking news. Psychologists have studied the accuracy of these kinds of memories and whether gender and age have an effect on remembering details. Suggest that interested students use the key words *flashbulb memory* to research this topic.

Exercise B. | Building Vocabulary

- Students complete the sentences with words from the box. Encourage them to try to match words with the context before looking words up in a dictionary.

- Compare answers as a class.

Answer Key

1. assumptions 2. desperate 3. intervene 4. compelled
5. conceived

Word Partners

When you *assume* something is the case, you think it is true even though you don't have proof for it. Therefore, you are guessing something or taking it for granted. Often stereotypes—widely held and oversimplified beliefs—underlie assumptions, hence they are called *common assumptions*.

Note that *assumption* often occurs in the set phrase *make assumptions about*, as in the first sentence of exercise **B.**

Vocabulary Notes

The two target vocabulary items *devise* and *conceive* have similar meanings when they refer to developing a mental plan to do something. Synonyms would be *formulate, invent,* and *dream up. Conceive* also means to understand or apprehend mentally. *Marcia couldn't conceive what her boss said about moving to New Zealand.*

Exercise C. | Using Vocabulary

- Ask students to think about answers to the questions before talking with a partner about them.
- Ask pairs to share their responses with the class.

Answer Key

Answers will vary, but note that when a person is *compelled* to do something, they are forced, driven, or obliged to act. Sometimes the force is internal, but often it's a matter of duty or responsibility. *The kindergarten teacher was compelled to report the bullying she saw.*

Exercise D. | Brainstorming

- Students work in groups of three or four to discuss the question.
- Have students explain what they thought initially and what led them to make those assumptions. Ask: *What led you to change your mind about a place?*

Answer Key

Answers will vary. Note that item 3 in exercise **C** is about a person, while this exercise focuses on first impressions of a place.

Exercise E. | Predicting

- Have students read the first two paragraphs of the reading and predict what will happen next in the story.
- Check their answer *after* students read the passage.

 track 2-04 You may want to play the audio while students read. Remind students that the vocabulary definitions in the numbered footnotes at the bottom of pages will help them understand the reading.

Overview of the Reading

Sebastian Junger is a journalist who has traveled widely and written articles and books and produced a documentary film about places he has experienced. The reading passage describes an incident during a cross-country hitchhiking trip in the United States. Later in the passage Junger recalls another winter trip, that time in the mountains of Spain, where he meets a memorable character. Later, he describes an encounter with a woman in a fishing town whom he is hesitant to approach. Junger says the people he has met have taught him important things that still influence his life and work.

Background

Sebastian Junger grew up in New England, on the east coast of the United States. After attending college, he started writing for newspapers while supporting himself working in a restaurant. Ever interested in travel, he sometimes traveled with a friend, but more often alone. In the reading passage, he is a "backpacker" who travels lightly with his clothes and equipment in a pack as he hitchhikes rides.

Junger has written several well-received books, especially *The Perfect Storm,* the account of a shipwreck that he refers to in the reading passage. As a journalist, Junger has covered conflict in Sierra Leone, Nigeria, Kosovo, and Afghanistan. His work includes a documentary film, *Restrepo,* about a military unit in Afghanistan. The film has won several awards.

Junger's original article from which the reading passage was taken can be found at **http://www .nationalgeographic.com/adventure/0605/features/ sebastian_junger.html**

IDEAS FOR . . . Checking Comprehension

Ask students the following questions about the reading.

What is Junger's initial attitude towards the people he meets on his travels? What kinds of things change his mind? What does he learn from the people he meets?

Understanding the Reading
45 mins

(pages 199–201)

Check students' predictions in exercise **E** on page 193.

Answer Key

Answers will vary. The photograph on page 194 shows the isolated setting of the first story. The first two paragraphs of the passage vividly portray a bleak place and describe a man who seems desperately poor. The writer is concerned about the man's intentions, so he has pepper spray to defend himself against attack. Students might predict that things don't go well for the writer.

Before proceeding with the comprehension questions, ask the class if there were areas of the reading that they didn't understand. Write the letters of the paragraphs or problematic vocabulary on the board and return to them if they are not clarified in the comprehension activities.

Exercise A. | Identifying Purpose

- Ask students to read the questions. If necessary, have them look back at the passage and reread the relevant paragraphs. Note: Information may be found in two or more paragraphs.

- Check the answers as a class and ask students to explain their choices by referring to lettered paragraphs in the text.

Answer Key

1. The text indicates that Junger has written a book and traveled in Spain and across the United States. In paragraph D, he says he has some expensive camping gear, so perhaps he is not poor. In paragraph O, he says he has covered wars as a journalist.

2. He wanted to tell people not to rely on first impressions or stereotypes. In many places, strangers or newcomers are suspect until local people find out about them. The distrust and uncertainty work both ways, but often strangers are welcome.

3. Basically he learned not to make assumptions about people and places. He stresses the importance of treating each person with respect.

Exercise B. | Identifying Purpose and Structure

Writers think carefully about structuring their work so that it conveys their purpose. This exercise requires students to analyze the purpose of five sections of the text.

Answer Key

1. e 2. c 3. d 4. a 5. b

Exercise C. | Identifying Key Details

- Allow time for students to write their answers individually.

- After students complete the exercise, check answers as a class. Invite volunteers to say where they found the answers to the items.

NOTE: Throughout this teacher's guide, letters in brackets are used to indicate the paragraph(s) where the answer is found.

Answer Key

1. Junger thought he was homeless, desperate, and possibly dangerous. [B]
2. Junger thought the man wanted food. [D]
3. He was surprised by the man's true generosity. [I]
4. Be wary, but open. Most of all, have respect for others. [J]
5. Don't make assumptions; keep your heart open; no one is better than anyone else. [K]
6. Respect everyone as having unique life experience and something to say. [L]
7. The man who stopped in the snowstorm in Spain to pick up a stranger [M and N]
8. He remembered the lessons from the other people and decided to just tell her that she had something special to say to the world (about losing her son in a shipwreck). [Q]

Exercise D. | Identifying Meaning from Context

- Encourage students to find the words or expressions and guess what they mean in the context of the lettered paragraph. Only then should they return to the page and complete the sentences.

- Students might want to create new sentences using these items for their vocabulary notebook.

Answer Key

1. f 2. e 3. b 4. a 5. c 6. d

CT Focus: Making Inferences about a Text

Go over the information in the **CT Focus** box. Writers often imply background information through descriptions or dialogue. Therefore, readers need to infer or deduce information that is not explicitly stated.

Exercise E. | Critical Thinking: Making Inferences

- Pairs of students work together to answer the questions by "reading between the lines" in the passage. They should note the words that suggest a particular interpretation.

- Compare responses as a class, asking students to support their ideas with examples.

Answer Key

Answers will vary, but here are some suggestions:

1. Junger felt embarrassed and guilty about taking food from someone who had less than he did, especially after initially thinking the man wanted his food and Junger hadn't wanted the man to know what he had. [C–H]
2. He wanted the firsthand experience of traveling rough and meeting people and learning lessons. [I–K]
3. He was probably in his twenties. He refers to the past with "I learned a lot in college" and says things like "aimless trips of my youth" and "as I got older. . . ." [I and O particularly]
4. He's doing it for protection because some people will take advantage of a sole traveler who is hitchhiking. He keeps it nearby in his pocket, so he clearly is a bit apprehensive. [B] You have to be wary and you have to protect yourself. [J]
5. He seems to be brave, open to adventure, willing to rough it, and respectful of others he encounters. [K, M, O, P]

Exercise F. | Critical Thinking: Personalizing

The goal of the exercise is for students to relate Junger's experiences to their own lives. In discussing with a partner whether they would like to travel as Junger does, ask about the advantages and disadvantages of traveling alone. Alone, you have more flexibility, and strangers are probably more likely to talk with you. When you travel with another person, you may be safer and also you have someone with whom to share your experiences.

Answer Key

Answers will vary according to students' personal travel experiences and preferences.

TIP These days, many solo travelers maintain travel blogs or use Twitter to document their journeys as well as share their experiences. Suggest that students read some travel blogs as a way of responding to the questions in exercise F. Search on key words *travel blogs* or visit National Geographic at http://www.nationalgeographic.com/ng-blogs/

45 mins

Developing Reading Skills
(page 202)

Reading Skill: Analyzing a Personal Narrative

Review the information in the **Reading Skills** box. A personal narrative is quite different from academic writing. When someone tells their own story, they can be subjective and use a range of descriptive words that make the reader able to visualize the setting and characters and to empathize with the storyteller. However, personal narratives still have a central theme or point that the writer is trying to express, and all the examples are used to support that theme.

Exercise A. | Analyzing

- Students look for examples of the main components of a personal narrative.

- As pairs of students work together to find examples, they should prepare to share their answers with the class.

Answer Key

1. **Setting:** There are three main settings: a road outside Gillette, Wyoming, the mountains near Salamanca in western Spain, and a pub in Gloucester (pronounced GLOSS ter), Massachusetts.
2. **Theme:** The theme is to not make assumptions and to respect everyone, whatever their role in life.
3. **Mood:** Junger shifts the mood as he tells his story. At first, he is suspicious and wary as he encounters the homeless man, then he is contrite. (Words and phrases used include *desperate, put my hand on the pepper spray, I was ready, alone and exposed, ripe for the pillage, sag with understanding,* and *learn true generosity.*) His mood also changes in the Spanish story from despondent to incredulous that someone would care for a stranger. (Words and phrases used include *I was in over my head, snowing hard, completely deserted, the only plan, I wondered,* and *and yet he took a risk.*) In the Gloucester pub, he is nervous and anxious. (Words and phrases used include *confronted, daunting, everyone turns to look,* and *no idea how to begin.*) In the sections where he looks back, he is appreciative of what he has learned.
4. **Characters:** Junger appears to be a capable young man, experienced as a traveler, and curious about the world. The homeless man seems dirty, unkempt, and yet incredibly generous.

Exercise B. | Retelling an Anecdote

Students use a time line to retell one of the two short stories in the reading passage. Remind the class that the oldest items go on the left side and the most recent ones on the right side.

IDEAS FOR . . . Expansion

National Geographic has many personal narratives. Another by Junger recounts his time in Sierra Leone. It is found at **http://www.nationalgeographic.com/adventure/sebastian-junger/fear-sierra-leone.html**

In the adventure section, located at **http://adventure.nationalgeographic.com/adventure/**, are many tales from travelers as well as professional adventurers. Some travelers tell amazing survival stories at **http://www.nationalgeographic.com/adventure/your-story/survival-stories.html**

Every year, *National Geographic* presents a photo gallery to document and recognize the journeys of outstanding adventurers. To learn more and see photos of the places, see **http://adventure.nationalgeographic.com/adventure/adventurers-of-the-year/2014/photos/**

Viewing: Frontline Diary
(page 203)

Overview of the Video

Iranian photojournalist Reza Deghati accompanies Sebastian Junger to an interview with Ahmad Shah Massoud, leader of the Northern Afghan Alliance, a group who opposed the Taliban. Massoud arranged to bring the men into Afghanistan secretly in an old helicopter. The situation was very dangerous, and on September 9, 2001, Massoud was assassinated. National Geographic cinematographer Stephen Cocklin did the video. Junger later wrote about this experience in a collection of articles called *Fire*. Film footage was also used in a National Geographic film, *Into the Forbidden Zone*, from which this video was excerpted.

Background Note

Some journalists specialize in reporting from war zones. While they themselves are in danger, the people they interview are as well, since they often represent dissident groups who seek regime change.

National Geographic was an important partner in the making of the documentary film, *Restrepo*, in Afghanistan. For more information about making the film, see **http://movies.nationalgeographic.com/movies/restrepo/junger-hetherington/**

Before Viewing

Exercise A. | Using a Dictionary

- Have students work individually to match the words and their definitions.
- Compare the answers as a class.
- Ask students to predict how these words will be used in the video.

Answer Key

1. smuggle 2. inaccessible 3. shrouded in mystery
4. chaos

Vocabulary Notes

A *shroud* is literally a piece of fabric that covers something up, such as cloth wrapped around a dead person before burial. Used figuratively, *shroud of mystery* refers to something that is obscured or hidden from view by things that are not fully understood.

Exercise B. | Thinking Ahead

In Unit 7, Diamond wrote about the influence of geography and history in Africa; these are important factors in Afghanistan as well. The landlocked country is located at the crossroads of Central, South, and West Asia and has been impacted by the cultures surrounding it. The high mountains of the Hindu Kush and Pamirs are only accessible through a few passes such as the Khyber. Afghanistan has a long history of foreign interference and warfare. In the 19th century, the British Empire and Russia fought to control it. After World War II, the USSR and the United States were opposing forces there. Civil war has been constant since the 1990s, especially with the reactionary Taliban forces. This has resulted in over a million deaths and millions of refugees.

On the UN's Human Development Index, Afghanistan is the 15th lowest country in the world in terms of life expectancy, GNI, and education. Development has suffered from warfare and lack of foreign investment.

While Viewing

- Ask students to read the questions so they are prepared to watch and listen for certain information. They should underline the key information in each question.
- Play the video while students write short answers to the questions.
- If necessary, play the video again, pausing it at each relevant item.

After Viewing

Exercise A.

Pairs of students discuss their answers.

Answer Key

1. remote, majestic, shrouded in mystery
2. They are smuggled in on an old rusty helicopter. They are traveling through a war zone and also they are flying by sight over high mountains without radar or landing lights.
3. as a ritual
4. He says they are incredibly generous, even when they hardly have any food.

Exercise B. | Critical Thinking: Synthesizing

By the time Junger went to Afghanistan, he had covered warfare and conflict in many places, so he was not surprised by the level of violence. However, he was impressed by the physical magnificence of the country. As in the reading passage, Junger was very moved by the generous attitude of the refugees.

IDEAS FOR . . . Expansion

Sebastian Junger is more than an author; he remains actively involved with people in the communities he writes about. For example, after writing *The Perfect Storm* about fishermen lost at sea, Junger started a foundation for the education of children whose parents are commercial fishermen.

His own Web site at **http://www.sebastianjunger.com/** is called the Official Sebastian Junger Community and contains links to all of the causes and groups he supports. These include war veterans and tragedy survivors. Some of his unpublished works are also on the site.

He made the documentary film *Restrepo* with his friend and photographer Tim Hetherington. Since Tim was killed covering conflict in Libya in April 2011, Junger has used his Web site to channel donations to charities in his memory. In addition, students may be interested to know that Junger made a documentary film about his friend's life, *Which Way Is the Front Line From Here?*

Exploring Written English
(page 204–206)

45 mins

- Read aloud the writing goal. Personal narratives often center on an experience that has great meaning for the individual.
- Remind students that writing is a process. Just as there are stages of reading or viewing that lead to comprehension, there are stages in the writing process that lead to producing a final draft. The lesson starts with a review of language for writing, and then it presents the steps in the writing process.
- Remind students about the Independent Student Handbook at the back of their Student Book. Pages 246–248 have useful tips on academic writing and research. On page 250, there is a chart of simple and past participle forms of irregular verbs.

Exercise A. | Brainstorming

- Students recall past experiences that taught them a valuable lesson. They share accounts of these stories and lessons with a partner.
- As they talk, students should note their partner's reaction. Ask: *Which story was most interesting or unusual? Was it interesting because it had enough details so that it seemed "real" to your partner?*

Exercise B. | Vocabulary for Writing

- This section contains time words that mark the sequence of events in a narrative.
- Make four columns on the board and label them *start, follow on, finish,* and *looking back.* Ask the class to sort the words into the four categories. Keep in mind that students will write their narrative from a present point of view, looking back at a formative event that occurred earlier.

Answer Key

Students' sentences will vary. For categorization of words, these are suggestions: ***start:*** at first, before; ***follow on:*** after, after that, during, from . . . to, later, meanwhile, next, the next time, then, whenever, while, until; ***finish:*** eventually, finally; and ***looking back:*** now.

Free Writing

- Remind students that free writing is writing rapidly to come up with ideas without worrying about mistakes.
- Set a time limit of five minutes for students to free write about an experience that taught a valuable lesson. Encourage students to use time markers from exercise **B**.

Exercise C.

- Go over the information and examples in the **Language for Writing** box.
- Remind students that in writing about past events, sometimes events occur at different times. To clarify when to use the simple past, the past continuous, and the past perfect, it can be helpful to draw a diagram to show the sequence of events. Use a different symbol for events that continued for a period of time as contrasted to those that were completed at one point. In the case of the past perfect, it is important to decide which event happened first.
- Students use the time clues to form sentences combining past tense forms.

Answer Key

1. I was hiking up a dusty trail when I encountered a rattlesnake.
2. Belmont had become a busy working-class town by the time I was born.
3. I had not really known the importance of trust until I started to spend a lot of time traveling.
4. We had gone on vacation to Wyoming three times before we moved there last year.

Writing Skill: Using Sensory Details

- Have students read the information in the box.
- The whole purpose of writing a personal narrative is to share an experience with readers. Therefore, the more colorful and evocative the language, the greater chance that the reader will be able to visualize the experience and identify with it.

Exercise D. | Critical Thinking: Analyzing

Students tell about the connotations of the underlined words and how they develop Junger's story.

Answer Key

1. *Desolate* is related to *deserted,* so the word conveys a sense of emptiness or bleakness, of being all alone. The photo on page 194 conveys that feeling too. When Junger is in that setting, he feels alone.
2. When a freight truck *barrels* past, it is moving very fast and the driver probably doesn't even notice the surroundings, including the hitchhiker by the side of the road.
3. When the bottles *explode,* the glass shatters violently and scatters fragments all over the place. This must have created a startling noise and a sense of violence.
4. The description of the homeless man *working his way* along means that he did it with great effort. Perhaps he had physical problems or maybe he was very cold or old. Movement was not easy for him.
5. When something is *filthy,* it is extremely dirty to the point that it smells and it is disgusting. Junger is using an extreme word to describe how unkempt the man is. *Matted* means extremely tangled and also conveys the sense of being unkempt. *On the skids* means in a bad situation and again conveys that the man is in desperate shape.
6. In some places, the end of daylight is sudden; it seems as though the clouds have gathered together and blotted out the remaining daylight. *Quickly gathering dusk* conveys the urgency Junger had to come up with a plan for the night.

Exercise E. | Critical Thinking: Applying

Students re-write five of their free-writing sentences using sensory details. Ask a partner to read the reworked sentences and underline the recently added words.

Writing Task: Drafting
(page 207)

Exercise A. | Planning

- This planning chart is a useful way to organize ideas before writing.
- Go over the five steps in the exercise.
- Point out that complete sentences are not necessary for the details and notes in the planning chart. The important thing is to get some ideas down on paper.
- For step 3, organize the sequence of events using a timeline such as the one on page 202.
- Allow time for students to complete their charts.

Exercise B. | Draft 1

- As students write their first draft, walk around and offer help as needed. It is not necessary to correct grammar at this stage.
- You may want to set this task for homework.

Writing Task: Revising
(pages 208–209)

Exercise C. | Critical Thinking: Analyzing

- Explain that analyzing this model essay will help students to revise their own writing.
- Allow time for students to work in pairs.

Answer Key

1. The first paragraph gives information about the writer's family background, their values, and his education and attitude towards work.
2. The thesis statement is "It doesn't matter what you do, just do the best you can." Yes, it explains what the writer learned.
3. The time words by paragraph are: 1. *when I was a child . . .*; 2. *It was January . . . for about a month . . . immediately;* 3. *After a few weeks, for a couple more nights, previous day, when I was in my early 20s;* 4. *When I was just about to give up, the entire time;* 5. *after that call, earlier, when I entered, right away, later;* 6. *a few weeks before, eventually, that winter*
4. Sensory words by paragraph: 1. *glamorous;* 2. *coldest, fantastic;* 3. *countless, patronizing, shivered;* 4. *ashamed, defeated;* 5. *posh-looking, massive, harried*
5. In the conclusion, the author reflects on his change in attitude.

Exercise D. | Revising

Explain that these steps will help students to reread their work carefully and look for ways to improve it.

Exercise E. | Peer Evaluation

- Explain that this process will help students to see if they have organized their ideas clearly.

- Discuss the four steps in the evaluation process to make sure students know what to do.

- Ensure that both members of the pair have equal time to give feedback.

Writing Task: Editing
(page 210)

Exercise F. | Draft 2

Walk around and monitor students as they work. Provide assistance as needed.

Exercise G. | Editing Practice

- Go over the information in the box.

- Allow time for students to find and correct the mistakes.

- Invite volunteers to write the corrected sentences on the board.

Answer Key

1. As soon as I arrived in Mexico City, I realized I had forgotten all the Spanish I had ever learned.
2. I was waiting at the bus stop when a friendly-looking older man stopped and asked me if I wanted a ride.
3. I learned that I had not applied for a passport early enough to go on my trip at the end of the month.
4. I was looking for the exit when suddenly all the lights went out.

Exercise H. | Editing Checklist

- Read aloud the sentences in the editing checklist.

- Allow time for students to read and edit their work.

Exercise I. | Final Draft

- Allow time for students to work on their final draft (or set this for homework).

- Collect students' work.

- Let them know when they can expect to get their essays back. At that time, be sure to go over the marking system that you use.

IDEAS FOR . . . Follow Up

After students finish their essays, have students write a one-sentence description of what they learned from the experience. Post the list of sentences on the notice board and have students try to guess who contributed each sentence. Use this as a team-building exercise in class to get students to be aware of others who may share similar viewpoints.

Imagining the Future

Academic Track
Interdisciplinary

Academic Pathways:
Lesson A: Reading literature critically
Identifying literary elements
Lesson B: Writing critically about literature
Writing an analysis of fiction excerpts

Unit Theme

Unit 10 explores the scientific and fictional perspectives of living in space beyond planet Earth. While several of the unit components deal with life on Mars, others explore exoplanets and the idea that life beyond our solar system is viable.

5 mins

⏱ Think and Discuss *(page 211)*

Ask students to describe the drawing. Ask: *Does the person in the drawing look like someone from Earth? Why or why not?* (His ear shape and large head and eyes vs. body proportions seem strange.) *What is he doing?* (Perhaps he is guiding a spaceship.) *What is the scene outside the window?* (There seem to be vehicles racing and crashing in the background.)

Background Note

The illustration is by Anthony Fiala, an American explorer, journalist, and photographer. He was educated as a designer and at one time drew cartoons. In the early 1900s, he went on several expeditions to the north pole. In 1914, he participated in an expedition to unexplored parts of Brazil with Theodore Roosevelt, formerly president of the United States.

- Survey the class for answers to question 1 and write responses on the board. Use this as a way of probing the background knowledge and interest of the class. The colonization of other planets—Mars in particular—has moved from being a science fiction topic to becoming an actual plan.

- The second question is also subjective, so answers will vary. Ask: *What kinds of people are interested in interplanetary exploration? Is this a dream or are people actually planning trips or expeditions?*

- A Dutch company called Mars One is planning an expedition in 2023. Over 100,000 people have applied to go, of which only 4 will be chosen. The intent is to establish a permanent colony on Mars. NASA, the American space agency, sent two unmanned probes to Mars in 2004 and hopes to send astronauts there in the 2030s. One of their main concerns is human exposure to radiation on the journey.

- Discuss the meaning of the unit title and how it relates to the illustration. In the title, *imagining* means thinking about the future and forming a mental plan. Thanks to space probes like the Mars rovers, scientists now have detailed and realistic information about other planets to use in planning.

15 mins

⏱ Exploring the Theme *(pages 212–213)*

The opening spread features capsule histories of the genre of science fiction superimposed on an artist's drawing meant to illustrate Ray Bradbury's *The Martian Chronicles*.

- Allow time for students to individually examine the drawing and read the text boxes.

- Then have students work with a partner to find answers to the questions.

- Start a class discussion by asking about the drawing. Ask: *What parts of it seem realistic? What seems like a fantasy? Why?* (At the present time, there seems to be no water on the surface of Mars, so the rivers or canals seem unreal. Also, it's not evident how the two people are breathing without special equipment in the thin atmosphere. Furthermore, the climate on Mars can be extreme, so why are the people so lightly clothed?) Ask about the buildings: *What are the buildings? How do people get from place to place?*

- Discuss the questions as a class.

- For question 2, ask if anyone has read any of the books mentioned.

Answer Key

Possible answers:

1. It was a time of scientific discovery and exploration of the Earth. Explorers found people with different cultures and ways of life, so extending these ideas to other planets seemed reasonable.
2. Students may be familiar with recent films and television series.
3. Developments in film technology have resulted in very dramatic portrayals of life in space. Actual space exploration such as the space shuttles, International Space Station, and men reaching the moon have led to science fiction that seems realistic. This trend will increase with actual attempts to colonize Mars and conduct probes of outer space in search of habitable exoplanets.

IDEAS FOR . . . Expansion

A textbox on page 212 mentions H. G. Wells's *The War of the Worlds,* written at the end of the 19th century. The book tells about the adventures of two brothers when Martian aliens invade England. The novel generated analytical literature that examines its place within contemporary ideas such as evolutionary theory, British Imperialism, and European political tensions about invasions.

A 1938 adaptation of the novel by Orson Welles caused widespread panic when it was presented as a radio broadcast. The program simulated a news broadcast and many listeners believed that Martians were actually invading the United States. Interested students can find out more about the science fiction novel and the broadcast by using the title or *Martian invasion* as search terms. They can also listen to MP3 files of the broadcast or watch a NASA commentary from 1975 at **https://archive.org/details/gov .archives.arc.649442**

Preparing to Read
(page 214–215)

30 mins

WARM-UP

A paragraph about the power of science fiction presents some target vocabulary in context.

The paragraph identifies a key attraction of science fiction: that it is both familiar and strange at the same time. We can attribute its familiarity to writers who

start with what they know about their own world and extend that to alien worlds built in their imaginations.

Exercise A. | Building Vocabulary

- Have students find the words in blue in the reading and use the other words around them to guess their meanings.
- Remind students that looking at the part of speech can help them figure out the meaning. Clues from surrounding words identify the part of speech. A candle *flickers,* with the word used as a verb, but in this paragraph *flickering* is an adjective. Similarly, *invasion* is usually a noun, but here it is used as an adjective.
- Allow time for students to complete the exercise individually.

Vocabulary Notes

A *sequel* is a book, play, or film that continues a story or situation presented in a previous work. For example, *The Empire Strikes Back* is a sequel to earlier films in the *Star Wars* series. A *prequel* is a neologism or new word formed by adding the prefix *pre-* to the base of sequel to describe a work written after the main work, but which gives the back story on which the main work is based. Ask the class about which of the *Star Wars* films were sequels and which were prequels.

Answer Key

1. look familiar
2. vanished
3. invasion
4. Sequels
5. Destiny
6. flickering

Exercise B. | Building Vocabulary

- Students complete the sentences with words from the box. Encourage them to try matching words using the context before looking words up in a dictionary.
- Compare answers as a class.

Answer Key

1. resembles
2. flee
3. stunned
4. in proportion
5. literally
6. dwindle

Word Link

Ask the class how the root word *liter* functions in the words given. *Alliteration*: repeating or adding the same letter or sound at the beginning of a word; *illiterate*: unable to read or write, can't make and understand letters; *literal* and *literally*: having the exact or primary meaning of words. Then ask the class about *literature* (written works like novels or poetry) and *obliterate* (to make something undecipherable so it cannot be read, later extended to mean destroying something completely).

Word Partners

The words collocated with *flee* usually have a negative connotation because when someone flees, they escape a dangerous situation. The simple past tense and participle is *fled*.

Exercise C. | Using Vocabulary

- Ask students to think about answers to the questions before talking with a partner about them.
- Ask pairs to share their responses with the class.

Answer Key

Answers will vary, but here is a suggestion:

1. The film *2001: A Space Odyssey,* based on a science fiction short story by Arthur Clarke, has a spaceship somewhat like recent space shuttles, but several crew members have been frozen in a state of cryogenic hibernation, and the spaceship is controlled by a computer named Hal. These latter two details are very different from space travel as we know it today.

Exercise D. | Brainstorming

Have students work in small groups to answer the questions.

Answer Key

Answers will vary, so here are some possible responses.

1. Organizations such as NASA are already conducting space exploration; it is a reality now.
2. for adventure, to start over in a new place, to take part in an experiment

Exercise E. | Predicting

- Students skim the reading on pages 216–222, noting that there are two distinct passages.
- Check answers *after* students read the passage.

 track 2-05 You may want to play the audio while students read. Remind students that the vocabulary definitions in the numbered footnotes at the bottom of pages will help them understand the reading.

Overview of the Reading

The first part of the reading passage is an autobiographical segment about how Ray Bradbury's interest in science fiction developed. As a boy, he read books about Mars by Edgar Rice Burroughs and wrote sequels to them. At 15, a science fiction film had a great impact on him. He continued to write, and an editor suggested that he combine his short stories into a novel called *The Martian Chronicles.* The second part of the reading passage is composed of excerpts from three of these stories. They tell of people who have left Earth to colonize Mars. After settling there for several years, the colonists witness a series of disasters on their former planet. Coded messages tell the space migrants to return to Earth.

Twenty-six years after writing *The Martian Chronicles,* Bradbury watched the first photographs come back from the Viking probe landing on Mars. In an interview, Bradbury asserted that people from Earth can go to Mars and become Martians.

> **IDEAS FOR . . . Checking Comprehension**
>
> Ask: *What were some of the main influences on Ray Bradbury? Did he believe that one day people from Earth would settle on Mars? Explain.*

> **IDEAS FOR . . . Expansion**
>
> *The Martian Chronicles* was published in 1950. A Web site devoted to Bradbury is at **http://www.raybradbury.com/** and the University of Indiana has a site for the study of Bradbury's work and legacy at **http://iat.iupui.edu/bradburycenter/**

Developing Reading Skills *(page 223)*

45 mins

Check students' predictions in exercise **E** on page 215.

Answer Key

1. b. an autobiographical essay
2. a. a set of fictional stories

Before proceeding with the comprehension questions, ask the class if there were areas of the reading that they didn't understand. Write the letters of the paragraphs or problematic vocabulary on the board and return to them if they are not clarified in the comprehension activities.

Reading Skill: Identifying Literary Elements

Go over the information in the **Reading Skill** box, noting the five main literary elements. Point out that a plot description sometimes discusses the phases of the plot or at least it identifies the climax or turning point.

Exercise A. | Analyzing

Students match the elements with examples.

Answer Key

1. d **2.** b **3.** e **4.** a **5.** c

Exercise B. | Applying

Students complete the chart with information about a story or movie and use the chart to describe it. Issac Asimov's 1941 classic short story *Nightfall* is given as an example. If you decide to model the process using this story, you will find it online at **http://www.uni.edu/morgans/astro/course/nightfall.pdf**

Title	*Nightfall*
Main Character(s) (Protagonist)	A group of scientists headed by Aton, a religious cult member, and a newspaper reporter
Setting	A solar system where other suns/stars are not visible due to the six suns
Point of View	An omniscient outside observer
Theme	A conflict between science and religion in interpreting the darkness
Plot	A planet with six suns experiences total darkness every 2049 years. People go mad and start fires for light, resulting in the civilization being totally destroyed.

⏱ Understanding the Reading (pages 224–225)
45 mins

Exercise A. | Understanding Main Ideas

- Ask students to read the questions and then quickly skim the autobiographical section for responses.
- Check the answers as a class, asking students to explain their choices.

Answer Key

1. As a boy, Bradbury lived on a street named for an astronomer. He read books about Mars by Edgar Rice Burroughs and wrote sequels to them. At 15, Wells's science fiction film *Things to Come* had a great impact on him. Bradbury often thought of himself as a Martian.
2. Bradbury was not upset that Mars appears to be uninhabited because he believed that people from Earth would settle there.

Exercise B. | Identifying Key Details

Allow time for students to scan the reading for the information in the autobiographical section.

Answer Key

1. John Carter was the protagonist of the Edgar Rice Burroughs books about Mars. Carter, a pioneer on the Red Planet, gave instructions that Bradbury followed in identifying with Mars.
2. It was the Depression era and he couldn't afford to buy the sequels.
3. He met Wernher von Braun, the prominent space scientist, and saw the first photographs of Mars relayed back to Earth.

Exercise C. | Identifying Meaning from Context

- Encourage students to find the words or expressions and guess what they mean in the context of that paragraph. Only then should they return to the page and select the closest match.
- Students might want to create new sentences using these items for their vocabulary notebook.

Answer Key

1. d 2. a 3. b 4. f 5. e 6. c

CT Focus: Reading Literature Critically

Go over the information in the **CT Focus** box, which emphasizes that it is usual to read a passage more than once. In the first reading, you are swept along by the plot, the characters, and what they do and say. A second or subsequent reading can focus on how the work is constructed and more subtle aspects of the language. In the later reading, inferencing is very important.

Exercise D. | Critical Thinking: Reading Literature Critically

- Individual students should answer the questions themselves before discussing answers in a small group. This ensures that each student can contribute to the group discussion.

- After groups complete the exercise, check answers as a class, asking students to note the paragraph(s) where they found answers to the items.

NOTE: Throughout this teacher's guide, letters in brackets are used to indicate the paragraph where the answer is found.

Answer Key

The Settlers
1. "The Loneliness" was triggered by seeing the homeland disappear, probably for good. It would have been similar to people who migrated from Europe to North America or Australia or actually anyone who left home to permanently take up residence somewhere else. [R]
2. The writer is suggesting that each person had their own reasons for making the trip. Social scientists who work with migration say that there are both *push* and *pull* factors. Push factors are things such as poverty, conflict, or having no land that cause you to leave a place. Pull factors are new opportunities, making a fresh start, or simply adventure that attract you to another place. [R]

The Locusts
3. The first group was the pioneers who got things set up, whereas later large numbers of rockets came with additional settlers. They arrived en masse, and the perception was that they were like a swarm of locusts. Review the video in Unit 5 to recall what swarming is like. [T]
4. The men with hammers were engaged in *terraforming,* contouring the alien landscape until it resembled "home" and so that it would be habitable by people from Earth. The Martian landscape is very rugged with huge ravines, high mountains, and volcanoes. Moreover, terraforming also refers to modifying the atmosphere and temperature of a planet. [T] There are many instances on Earth where people changed the original landscape to make it more like home. In the process, they have often created irreparable damage, as Jared Diamond would be the first to point out.

The Watchers
5. Earth had become as distant to them as Mars once was, but they still had relatives there and were in communication enough to know that a war was starting. They were worried and initially tried to calm each other. As they received the messages to come home, their allegiance to their original planet came to the fore, and they bought suitcases to start their journeys. [V–Z]

Developing Reading Skills

45 mins

(page 226)

Exercise E. | Critical Thinking: Interpreting Figurative Language

The exercise gives guided practice in interpreting figurative statements in Bradbury's writing. Students discuss their ideas with a partner.

Answer Key

1. That is when Bradbury's commitment to Mars started and it never stopped.
2. Bradbury often refers to an "internal Martian" that is the muse for his writing.
3. People often identify themselves by naming where they are from. In some languages, there are markers as part of a surname that indicate your hometown. For example, Rembrandt van Rijn's family was from the Rhineland region. When hometown has no meaning, you become deracinated or rootless.
4. The rockets came in clusters, with a rhythm like a drum.
5. Carpenters on Earth often put nails in their mouth so they have both hands free to nail down a roof, for instance.
6. Fireflies shine intermittently, not steadily, so the Morse code with its dots and dashes seemed analogous to fireflies.
7. Being in space so far away had numbed them from concerns about Earth.

Exercise F. | Critical Thinking: Making Inferences

The exercise gives students a great deal of room to respond personally.

Answer Key

1. One interpretation is that Bradbury had a strong sense of dramatics—see paragraph P—and he liked to have his career regarded as destiny, that from boyhood he was meant to write about space travel and life.
2. Perhaps he played with Thomas Wolfe's idea about "you can't go home again" because resettlement on Mars was supposed to be permanent. Yet, despite the distance from Earth and all the difficulties there, the Martian settlers seem to be pulled back home.

IDEAS FOR . . . Expansion

Students may be interested in finding out more about the Dutch Mars One program at **http://www.mars-one.com/en/** or by searching on the key words *colonizing Mars.*

Alternatively, students could look through the student book for examples of terraforming on Earth and the consequences of making such changes. Some ideas to explore include the extensive terracing in Unit 1 and the desertification of the Sahel in Unit 7.

Viewing Mission: Mars

(page 227)

Overview of the Video

Several planetary scientists and a narrator talk on the video, mostly about features of the landscape on Mars. Most notable is the huge canyon 2500 miles long and 6 miles deep. Another outstanding feature is the highest mountain in the solar system, an extinct volcano called Olympus Mons, about 17 miles high.

Background Note

One of the narrators of the video is Steve Squyres, the principal investigator of the Mars Exploration Rover Mission. As an undergraduate, Squyres was a student of the late Carl Sagan and has returned to teach astronomy at his alma mater, Cornell University in New York state. Read what Squyres says about the exploration of Mars: **http://www.nationalgeographic.com/adventure/0602/whats_new/nasa_steve_squyres.html**

The Jet Propulsion Lab (JPL) branch of NASA (the U.S. Space Agency) has a Web site with lesson ideas for teachers at **http://marsrovers.jpl.nasa.gov/home/index.html** JPL searches for *exoplanets,* possibly habitable planets outside the solar system, using the high-power Kepler telescope. See **http://planetquest.jpl.nasa.gov/**

Before Viewing

Exercise A. | Using a Dictionary

- Have students work individually to match the words and their definitions.
- Compare the answers as a class.

Answer Key

1. fissure 2. colossal 3. scenery 4. gravity

Vocabulary Notes

There are many names for *canyons,* or deep gorges with steep cliff walls. Sometimes they are called ravines or valleys. Geologists think they were originally formed by rivers cutting through soft rock. This suggests that the colossal canyon on Mars originally held running water.

Exercise B. | Thinking Ahead

A huge canyon and an extinct volcano—the highest mountain in our solar system—are main features. Photographs from Mars spacecraft have shown impact craters from meteors as well as the two moons of Mars.

While Viewing

- Ask students to read the questions so they are prepared to watch and listen for certain information. They should underline the key information in each question.
- Play the video while students write short answers to the questions.

After Viewing

Exercise A.

- Have students work in pairs to discuss and compare answers.
- Ask students if there are any points that are unclear that they wish to discuss.

Answer Key

1. a huge canyon 2500 miles long and 6 miles deep
2. the enormous amount of water that must have flowed through it
3. three times higher than Everest
4. With lower gravity, things can pile higher.

Exercise B. | Critical Thinking: Synthesizing

He probably would have incorporated some of the information into his stories and made them even more dramatic.

Exploring Written English

(page 228–230)

45 mins

- Read aloud the writing goal.

- Remind students that writing is a process. Just as there are stages of reading or viewing that lead to comprehension, there are stages in the writing process that lead to producing a final draft. The lesson presents criteria for selecting and supporting an argument, reviews language for writing, and then presents the steps in the writing process.

- Remind students about the Independent Student Handbook at the back of their Student Book. Pages 246–248 have useful tips on academic writing and research. The common signal phrases on page 248 are especially useful in writing an analysis of literature.

Writing Skill: Writing Critically about Literature

The writing skill text emphasizes the importance of choosing an argument that is broad enough to include several argument points, each supported by quotes or paraphrases from the piece of writing.

Exercise A. | Critical Thinking: Evaluating

Students select the topics they think are broad enough to support an analysis.

Answer Key

The fullest topic is the first one, but statement four could also be expanded and developed with examples of why it is a cautionary tale. Statement two is too limited, and statements three and five are too general to be productive topics.

Exercise B. | Critical Thinking: Evaluating

Have someone read the argument out loud and then discuss the theme as a class. It should be clear that evidence should be connected to problems or difficulties.

Answer Key

Items two and six provide the strongest evidence for the argument, while items four and five also mention problems, albeit more subtly. Items one, three, and seven are off topic for the argument.

Language for Writing: Using a Variety of Sentence Types

The **Language for Writing** box reviews types of sentences with examples that demonstrate the features of each type.

Exercise C. | Analyzing

Students identify the types of sentences by looking for distinctive features.

Answer Key

1. This is a compound (CD) sentence of two independent clauses joined by *but*.
2. This is a complex (CX) sentence with a dependent clause starting with the relative pronoun *that*.
3. This is a complex (CX) sentence with an adverb clause starting with *as* meaning "during that time."
4. This is a simple (S) sentence.
5. This is a complex (CX) sentence with a dependent clause starting with the subordinator *because* that gives a reason or cause for their problems.

Exercise D. | Brainstorming

- Students work in pairs to think of three excerpts from *The Martian Chronicles* that support each of the two arguments.

- In both cases, suggestions are provided in parentheses.

Answer Key

Answers will vary, but here are some suggestions.

Topic 1: comparison of actions and feelings of people on Mars to real life
1. reasons for going to Mars in [R]
2. colonization process with pioneer group, later arrivals, loneliness in [R, S, and T]
3. the attempts to make Mars like home, despite the fact that it was very different in [T, U, and V]

Topic 2: examples of a reading passage as a cautionary tale
1. government recruitment of colonists who may have had diverse reasons for leaving Earth [R] and then the organized invasion of new arrivals [T]
2. time and distance don't erase memories or a sense of connection [V]
3. warfare and conflict aren't resolved by colonizing space [V through Y]

Free Writing

- Remind students that free writing is writing rapidly to come up with ideas without worrying about mistakes.

- Set a time limit of five minutes for students to free write about one of the topics they choose in exercise **A**. Note that the brainstorming activities in the previous exercise have generated possible excerpts to use for each of the acceptable topics.

Writing Task: Drafting

(page 231)

Exercise A. | Planning

- Point out that this planning chart is a useful way to organize ideas before writing.

- Go over the four steps in the exercise, noting that there will be an introduction, three body paragraphs, and a conclusion.

- Point out that complete sentences are not necessary for the details and notes in the planning chart. The important thing is to get some ideas down on paper.

- Allow time for students to complete their charts.

Exercise B. | Draft 1

- As students write their first draft, walk around and offer help as needed. It is not necessary to correct grammar at this stage.

- You may want to set this task for homework.

Writing Task: Revising

(pages 232–233)

Exercise C. | Critical Thinking: Analyzing

- Explain that analyzing this model essay will help students to revise their own writing.

- Encourage students to pay particular attention to how the author has used evidence in the body paragraphs.

- Additionally, draw students' attention to the highlighted areas and their comments.

Answer Key

1. The thesis statement is the last sentence in the first paragraph.

2. The topic sentences occur as the first sentences in paragraphs 2, 3, and 4.

3. Even the opening paragraph uses a quote to support the idea of the problems people are ostensibly leaving behind.

In paragraph 2, an extensive quote about Loneliness is used and expanded upon.

Paragraph 3 about the ugliness of Mars paraphrases the impact of the rockets landing and uses two direct quotes about "neon tubes and yellow electric bulbs" and "flowerpots and chintz" to support the idea that the settlers need to be surrounded by familiar things.

Paragraph 4 uses three direct quotes ("Earth now was dead," "explode, catch fire, and burn" and "COME HOME. COME HOME. COME HOME.") to support the idea that the colonists' problems haven't disappeared.

4. The last two sentences in the conclusion repeat the main point that you cannot escape your identity or problems.

Exercise D. | Revising

Students follow the same analytical steps as they reread their work carefully and look for ways to improve it.

Exercise E. | Peer Evaluation

- Remind students that this process will help students to see if they have organized their ideas clearly.

- Ensure that both members of the pair have equal time to give feedback.

Writing Task: Editing

(page 234)

Exercise F. | Draft 2

Walk around and monitor students as they work. Provide assistance as needed.

Exercise G. | Editing Practice

Students use the checklist to find and correct any errors.

Exercise H. | Final Draft

- Allow time for students to work on their final draft (or set this for homework).

- Collect students' work.
- Let them know when they can expect to get their essays back. At that time, be sure to go over the marking system that you use.

IDEAS FOR . . . Further Research

There are many useful Web sites on using science fiction in ESL/EFL classes. The sites suggest literature available in the public domain that students can access free online as well as follow-on activities including filming a video or creating illustrations for a story.

Our Human Impact

Complete the chart as you read *The Human Age*.

What is the issue?

Epoch
_____
Holocene
Pleistocene

Why does it matter?

"We are no longer in the _____"

Criteria for a new epoch

_____

_____

_____

_____

What will be lasting signs of human impact?

farming

1. nitrogen _____

2. _____

   _____

deforestation

1. sedimentation

2. loss of _____

atmosphere

1. global _____

a. _____ ranges

b. extinction

acidic oceans

1. _____ _____ warms the planet

2. reef _____

What will renaming do?

Crutzen's purpose:

"What I hope," he says, "is that the term *Anthropocene* will be a warning to the world."

What will this do?

Your ideas:

_____

_____

_____

_____

_____

_____

Conservation and Protection

Complete the chart as you read *A Cry for the Tiger* and watch the video, *Tigers in the Snow*. Be sure to use the map on page 33.

	Historically	Now
Numbers		
Locations		
Breeding areas		

List problems that tigers face now:

loss of _____

growth of the _____ population

poaching for _____

lack of _____ between breeding areas

logging in Siberia

Possible solutions:

patrol _____

set aside _____ areas where tigers are protected

create corridors between _____

_____

stop _____ in the forests

Beautiful

Use the graphics, photographs, and text from *Images of Beauty* to complete the information in the chart below.

Photographer or artist	Name of image	What the image shows	Why is it special?
Vincent van Gogh	The Bridge in the Rain	A _____ with people on it during the _____	It is like a _____ woodblock print
Sam Abell	Morning _____ at Kelly's Ford, Virginia		The special quality of _____ through a morning fog turns a forest into _____ _____
James Stanfield	_____ at the Louvre, _____	A child _____ for joy in a _____ at the Louvre Museum.	The important thing is the geometric _____ of the photograph.
Martin Kers	Tree lined road in the _____		It has a soothing _____ of yellows and greens.
Annie Griffiths	Time exposure of _____ speeding past a _____	The photograph was taken at _____ and you see a _____ on his _____	Because of time exposure, you do not see the _____ but only ribbons of _____
Rich Reid	Hugging, twisted _____		Good photography makes us pay attention to _____ things like _____

Powering Our Planet

Fill in the timeline as you read *Our Energy Challenge*.

When	What
2100 ↑	_____ levels could rise by six and a half feet.
2030 ↑	We need to stop burning _____ anywhere on _____.
2030 ↑	World energy consumption will _____ by _____ percent.
now ↑	We need to find sources of _____ other than fossil fuels.
2010 ↑	Twin problems: _____ oil and _____ warming.
2008 ↑	International Energy Agency: _____ production declining by _____ percent a year.
2007 ↑	The _____ melted.
2000 ↑	China starts to suffer from _____.
1990s ↑	Install _____ on smokestacks and catalytic _____ on exhaust pipes in the United States.
1980s to now ↑	The _____ and information revolutions.
1900s ↑	The chemical _____.
1700s and 1800s ↑	The _____ revolution with great clouds of _____ in London.
Start 18th century ↑	Started to use _____ to run engines.
Distant past	Used _____ and animal energy and _____ for sails.

Working Together

Read *The Smart Swarm* and the essay about social insects on page 116 and then complete the diagram.

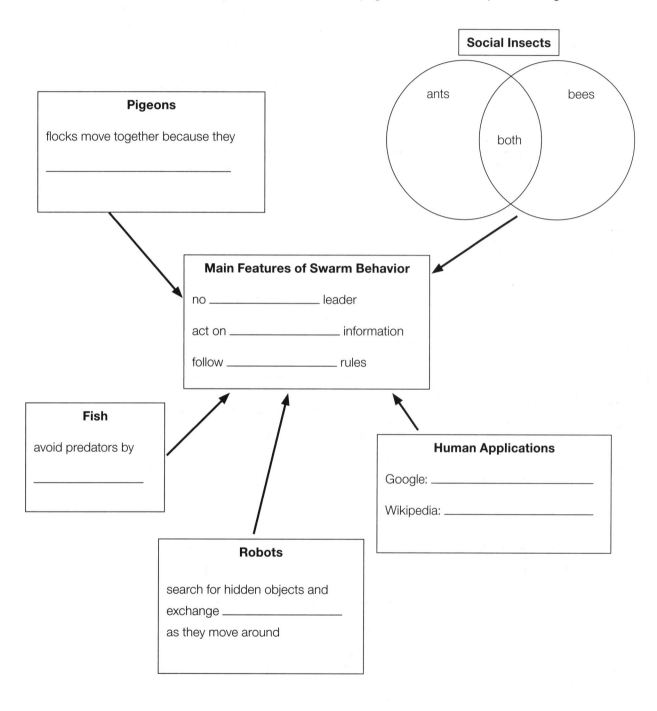

Pigeons

flocks move together because they

_____

Social Insects

ants

bees

both

Main Features of Swarm Behavior

no _____ leader

act on _____ information

follow _____ rules

Fish

avoid predators by

_____

Robots

search for hidden objects and

exchange _____

as they move around

Human Applications

Google: _____

Wikipedia: _____

Language and Culture

Read Daisy Zamora's autobiographical narrative *The Secret Language* and complete the chart.

Who and When	Influence on Language
Today she is a noted Latin American poet.	She writes in Spanish, but her poetry is _____ into many _____.
At university, she studied literature.	Some authors she read then were _____ _____.
She sometimes became discouraged trying to learn everyday English.	She read a _____ of Dostoevsky.
As a teenager, she visited her cousins in the United States.	They thought her English was _____, so she had to learn _____ English.
She collected music with English _____ like the Beatles and _____ Sinatra.	She learned the lyrics and sang along.
_____ classes were her favorite.	The language became _____, integral to her being and she absorbed it.
_____ movies and baseball were sources for English.	Her _____ used the language in games.
Daisy learned English from cartoons on TV.	She learned _____ from cartoons; characters said what they were _____.
Daisy went to school, kindergarten through third grade.	She learned to count _____ and read _____.
Daisy grew up as part of a large family in Nicaragua.	She heard some _____ from her grandmother.
Her grandmother at age 14 and her grandmother's family returned to Nicaragua.	They spoke _____ there but remembered _____ from New Orleans.
Her grandmother came to New Orleans from Europe to spend her childhood.	They spoke English and some _____.

Resources and Development

Read Jared Diamond's article *The Shape of Africa* and complete the chart.

Geographical issues:

Thick tropical core between two

_____ zones

few plants and animals suitable for

_____

continent oriented _____ – _____

mostly landlocked, only _____
River extends far inland

History:

Humans originated in Africa

Why didn't people domesticate plants and animals there?

_____

_____

Problems: (state why)

Disease:

Poverty:

Environmental issues:

desertification in the Sahel

Solutions: (state how)

Public health:

Use technology to be part of global economy

Take advantage of number of _____-speaking workforce

Use resources wisely

rivers:

animals:

forests:

Living Longer

Read *Beyond 100* and watch the video, *Secrets of a Long Life*. Then fill the chart with information.

Consider these kinds of factors: active life style, vegetarian diet, importance of social connections/family, no smoking or drinking, genetics and family history, belonging to a group (religious or social), medical care, attitude, luck, and caloric restriction.

Case Study Location	Characteristics of People	Kind of Research	Conclusions about Longevity Factors
Calabria, Italy		interviews documentary genetic	
Okinawa, Japan	biking/fishing group of friends		
Sardinia, Italy	role of women (effect?)	film crew	
Linda Loma, CA, U.S.	free Saturdays		

Memorable Experiences

Read *Welcome Stranger* and watch the video, *Frontline Diary*. Then fill in the Venn diagram about unique, shared, and common experiences.

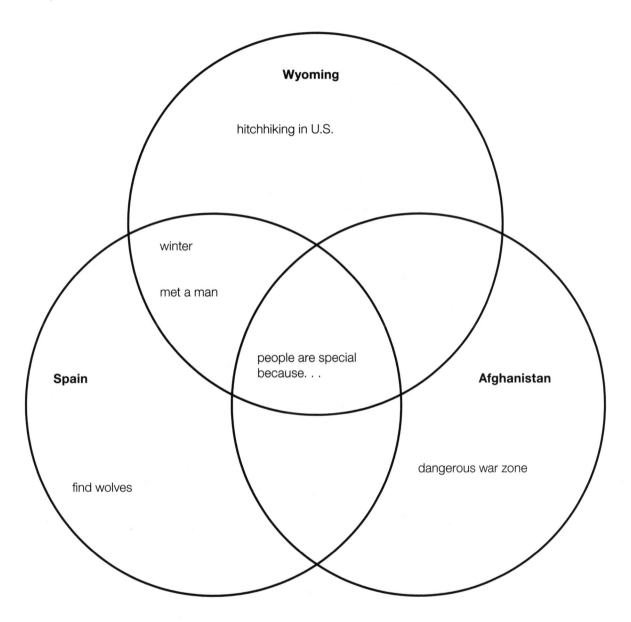

Wyoming

hitchhiking in U.S.

winter

met a man

people are special because. . .

Spain

Afghanistan

find wolves

dangerous war zone

Imagining the Future

Read the excerpts from Ray Bradbury's *The Martian Chronicles* and put these statements in sequence from 1 (earliest) to 10 (last).

_____ The men make the landscape look like home.

_____ The government decides to start a settlement on Mars.

_____ The colonists watch the war on Earth from Mars.

_____ Some people decide to go to Mars, but for a variety of reasons.

_____ The government recruits settlers for Mars, offering employment.

_____ People buy suitcases as they prepare to return to Earth.

_____ The first group of pioneers suffers from the Loneliness.

_____ People hear a radio broadcast that there are problems on Earth.

_____ Soon, settlers arrive in swarms of rockets that scorch the surface of Mars.

_____ A message in Morse code tells the people to return to Earth.

Then, write a summary using time markers such as *first*, *after that*, *next*, and *finally*.

_____

_____

_____

_____

_____

_____

_____

_____

_____

_____

_____

_____

_____